ETHICS IN COUNSELING and PSYCHOTHERAPY

PERSPECTIVES in ISSUES and DECISION MAKING

(*Includes the* ETHICAL JUDGMENT SCALE *and* MANUAL)

by

William H. VanHoose
Professor of Counselor Education,
University of Virginia

and

Louis V. Paradise
Assistant Professor of Counselor Education,
Catholic University of America

THE CARROLL PRESS
Publishers
Cranston, R. I. 02920

WILLIAM H. VAN HOOSE is professor in counselor education, University of Virginia, Charlottesville where he served as chairman of the department for three years. Previously he was professor and chairman of the department of counseling and guidance at Wayne State University and assistant professor of educational psychology, University of Michigan. He has also been a lecturer in education at the College of William and Mary, supervisor of child study and guidance in a large city school district, a counselor, school psychologist and counselor for juvenile offenders in a state department of mental health and corrections.

Dr. Van Hoose is author, co-author or editor of seven books and co-author or author of over thirty articles in professional journals. His books include *Counseling and Guidance in the Twentieth Century* and *The Authentic Counselor.* He has also contributed chapters to four books dealing with such topics as Children's Rights and Professionalism in Counseling. Several of his research reports have appeared in university publications.

Long active in professional associations, Dr. Van Hoose has chaired several state and national professional committees during the past five years. He holds a Ph.D. from Ohio State University, an M.S. from Indiana University and an A.B. from Morehead State University, Kentucky.

LOUIS V. PARADISE is assistant professor of counseling at Catholic University of America, Washington, D.C. Prior to his present position, Dr. Paradise was a clinical intern at the Adult Psychiatric Clinic of the University of Virginia Hospital and an instructor in lab practicum in counseling for master's level counselors at the University of Virginia.

Dr. Paradise is the author or co-author of one other book and numerous professional articles in the field of counseling and psychology. He maintains a private practice of psychology in Washington, D.C., and has served as a research consultant to several Washington-based consulting firms. He received his Ph.D. in counseling from the University of Virginia, an M.S. in psychology from Bucknell University, a diploma in Middle East and North Africa Studies from the Foreign Service Institute of the U.S. Department of State, and his B.S. from Pennsylvania State University.

Library of Congress Cataloging in Publication Data:

Van Hoose, William H.
    Ethics in counseling and psychotherapy.

    Bibliography: p.
    Includes index.
    1. Psychotherapy ethics. 2. Judgement (Ethics) — Testing.
I. Paradise, Louis V., joint author. II. Title. [DNLM: 1. Ethics, Medical.
2. Counseling. 3. Decision making. 4. Psychotherapy. WM62 V256e]
  RC455.2.E8V37   *174'.2*   *79-15429*   *ISBN 0910328-25*
Manufactured in the United States of America

CONTENTS

Ethics in Counseling and Psychotherapy

The Ethical Judgment Scale Manual

The Ethical Judgment Scale

PREFACE

It is now possible, and even probable, that many students in counseling and psychotherapy are obtaining degrees in one of these professions without ever having had more than one or two lectures on professional ethics. That is a serious omission in a program of professional preparation. No matter how well prepared a person may be, there is something missing unless the professional understands the impact of moral conduct upon counseling procedures and outcomes. We believe that this text can acquaint students with relevant ethical issues and their implications for the profession.

This book has two purposes: First, to help students and practitioners in counseling and psychotherapy examine some of the ethical issues and problems in the helping profession, and the second purpose is linked to this first one; the book is designed to serve as a text for teaching about ethics in the helping professions.

In the opening chapter we introduce the reader to the study of ethics and provide definitions of several terms pertinent to the general topic. Chapter Two discusses ethics in contemporary society and emphasizes the need for mental health professionals to understand the impact of moral standards and issues upon their work. Contributions from several ethical theorists are summarized in Chapter Three. Three theoretical approaches, hedonism, self-actualization, and moral developmentalism, have considerable relevance for ethical thinking and these positions are reviewed in some detail. Recent research on moral development and ethical decision making is reviewed in Chapter Four. The last chapter contains two major parts; the first consists of a discussion of current ethical issues in counseling and psychotherapy and the second part deals with ethical decision making and includes several case illustrations for those who wish to delve into the topic more deeply.

The authors have developed an *Ethical Judgment Scale* (EJS) which is also most appropriate for use in teaching about ethics in the helping professions. This companion work contains twenty-five incidents or case vignettes, covering ethical dilemmas in counseling and psychotherapy. The manual for the EJS explains the development of the scale and describes its use in teaching and research. The EJS will provide both instructors and students a useful complement to this text. Many of the concepts discussed appear in case form in the EJS. Thus, use of the two works provides an additional method for inquiry about some of the moral and ethical dimensions of counseling and psychotherapy.

The views presented are not original. We propose no new theories and offer no new approaches for dealing with moral issues. We have been influenced by several viewpoints and personalities; we still have much to learn.

Several people have assisted us in our work on the text and the Ethical Judgment Scale. Several valuable suggestions and insights were provided by Anna Askounis. The active cooperation and enthusiasm of our students in three universities has made these works possible. Our gratitude to them is profound. We are also grateful for the general assistance and typing of Becky Zellers and Barbara Howard.

WILLIAM H. VAN HOOSE
LOUIS V. PARADISE

This work is dedicated to —
Fred and Pam Van Hoose
and to
Christopher and Gabrielle Paradise

Chapter One

AN INTRODUCTION TO ETHICS

Can anyone now speak clearly of "right" and "wrong" actions? In a world trembling with change, are there any valid measures of "good" and "evil?" What are the standards that can be used for decision-making? Is ethics dead or alive in twentieth century America? These questions provide an appropriate starting point for our discussion of ethics in counseling and psychotherapy.

This text deals primarily with ethical problems and decision-making in the helping professions. The helping professions include counseling, psychology, social work, psychiatry and myriad related professions which provide professional psychological services such as helping people make decisions and solve problems.

We are aware that distinctions are often made between the terms, counseling and psychotherapy. We too recognize some differences particularly in terms of objectives and severity of the clients' problems. In an attempt at practicality, however, we use the terms *counseling* and *psychotherapy* synonymously. For the same reason we also use the terms *counselor* and *therapist* in a generic sense to refer to all psychological helpers.

This chapter provides an overview of the general topic and includes some definitions relevant to the study of ethics. We believe that some introductory statements are necessary for helping the reader understand what is to follow. In succeeding chapters we deal specifically with ethics in counseling and psychotherapy.

In his classical work *Reason in Ethics* Toulmin (1968), explains that ethics is a topic which holds some interest for everybody. Scientific theories and problems often intrigue us and occupy our thinking and discussion for short periods of time but generally science and technology interest only a small number of people. On the other hand everyone is interested in moral problems and human conduct. Further, most people must constantly deal with moral issues or problems that require action. So everyone is concerned about ethics.

This does not mean that the principles of right conduct or concepts of "good" and "bad" are perpetual topics of conversation – far
from it. Often the discussion is anything but explicit. Still, either
directly, or under another name, ethical concepts and ethical problems creep into our thoughts and our discussions.

During the past few years this concern about ethics has grown
considerably. Concurrently a steady stream of ethical literature and
moral oratory has flowed into the world. From books, television
screens, newspapers, legislative chambers, and pulpits we read and
hear discussions of "dishonesty," "cover-ups," "rights," "responsibilities," "common decency," "justice," and "injustice." Ethics committees investigating misconduct of government officials make head-
lines and the evening news. So the general public is quite aware of
ethics in contemporary society even though the term may not be
commonly used. One does not have to be an ethicist or a social
scientist to understand that some of the problems that wrack contemporary civilization are in fact ethical in nature.

These statements suggest that ethics, and an understanding of
ethical problems has considerable social relevance. Further, ethics
has another kind of importance as well, since it underlies much of
the work done in other fields, particularly the social sciences. For
example, when the political scientist speaks of "civil rights," sociol-
ogists of "racism," or psychologists of "abnormal personality,"
their language presupposes value concepts. If any one of the problems raised by use of these terms, or by scores of others, were to
be pursued far enough it would finally resolve itself into a problem
of ethics (Johnson, 1974).

The Meaning of Ethics

Several philosphers have defined ethics as a study of human
conduct. Ethics is also concerned with norms or standards and with
right and wrong behavior or actions. A distinction needs to be made
between *conduct* and *behavior*. Behavior, as used in the social sciences, refers to overt actions such as driving a car, making love, or
playing a guitar. Ethics is concerned with behavior but not with *all*
behavior equally. Ethics deals with that type of behavior more
appropriately called *conduct* where the person makes a voluntary
choice between alternative courses of action. Thus, conduct might
be called "moral" behavior where "moral" does not denote good/bad
behavior but behavior which results from a moral decision.

In his description of the subject matter of ethics, Moore (1971)
in *Principia Ethica* noted that it is relatively easy to identify matters
with which ethics are concerned. "Whenever we say, 'So and so is a

good man,' or 'That man is a crook,' and when we ask, 'What ought I to do?' or 'Is it wrong for me to do this?' and whenever we make such statements as, 'Temperance is a virtue and drunkeness a vice,' we are dealing with matters of ethics. In the vast majority of cases, where we make statements involving any of the terms, virtue, vice, duty, right, wrong, ought, good, or bad, we are making ethical judgments; and if we wish to discuss their truth, we shall be discussing a point of ethics."

It is appropriate at this point to distinguish between ethics and morality. Mowrer (1967) uses the terms interchangeably but suggests that *moral* refers to the goodness or badness of a behavior while *ethics* is an objective inquiry about behavior. Johnson (1974) also recognizes the difficulty of maintaining a distinction between these two terms. He suggests that "moral" or "morality" refers not to practice but to theory. Thus, one should not say that someone is ethically good; rather it should be said that the person is a good ethicist, meaning that the person's theories on ethics are sound. This difference in use of terms is not followed by the general public, however. Ethics is often used in place of moral and morality. For example we may speak of "unethical practices" when we refer to actions rather than to "immoral behavior." When we say that someone has the ethics of an alley cat we may be saying the person is morally corrupt while at the same time casting aspersions on legions of harmless alley cats. We recognize that "ethics" and "morals" are intricately connected. Ethics is a theoretical examination of morals or morality; overt behavior or conduct might be called "moral" or moral behavior. In this text we make frequent use of both terms when referring to human conduct. For present purposes we favor the term "ethics" since we will be discussing codes of ethics and ethical decision-making at some length. Moreover, we hope that the objectivity which we have attempted to bring to this work is more visible as a result of the use of the term "ethics."

The difference between an ethicist and a moralist should also be clarified. As noted previously the interest of the ethicist is theoretical; s/he is trying to understand morality and moral behavior. The moralist, on the other hand, is concerned with actions or overt behaviors. S/he wants people to improve their behavior. From what we have seen, the ethicist may have the easier task.

Some Ethical Questions

For several centuries moral philosophers have attempted to answer such questions as: "What things are good?" "What actions are appropriate?" "Is this alternative better than that?"

Clear thinking about the nature of these and other ethical questions soon reveals that solid evidence supporting any particular answer to these questions is not readily apparent. One of the first problems is that the questions are so unclear that we do not understand what we are seeking. It is the ancient "needle in the haystack" problem. Our first task then is to examine the questions and try to make them clearer either by defining terms or by providing explanations of their meaning. This is no simple problem. Consider for example the various definitions of "good," or try to determine the myriad views about "right actions."

It is obvious that many ethical questions are complex, some are vague, and most are laden with hypostatization and anthropomorphism. Nevertheless, it is necessary to raise these questions even when answers prove elusive and perhaps impossible to attain. For the process of inquiry is essential to the development of a set of principles for use in ethical reasoning and decision-making. An understanding of this process and the establishment of these principles is one of our main objectives.

Right and Wrong Acts

In Chapter Three we present several views on the notion of right and wrong actions. In this section it will suffice to briefly describe the essential elements of this concept.

Most of us believe that some actions are right and others wrong and that we have a duty to act on the former and to avoid the latter. Johnson (1974) writes that the duty to do what is right represents a unique kind of moral obligation, the presence of which is usually indicated in our everyday discourse by the appearance of the word "ought." When we say that someone "ought" to do such and such we are imputing a moral obligation to him/her. For example, if we say, "People should pay their debts," we are saying that it is a duty to pay debts and that it is the right action or the right thing to do. Conversely, when we say, "People ought to pay their debts," we are implying that it is wrong to fail to pay one's debts.

Not all "oughts" imply moral obligations. In some instances the term expresses necessity or desirability. For example, "You ought to see your dentist," may imply that if you do not you may lose your teeth but there is no moral obligation tied to a visit to the dentist. Similarly, "You ought to try sun bathing," suggests that this may be a pleasurable act but few people would suggest that sun-bathing is a duty or a necessity.

Several major philosophers have dealt at length with the notion of moral duty. The German philosopher Kant believed that actions of any sort must be undertaken from a sense of duty dictated by reason. No action performed solely for expediency or in obedience to law or custom can be regarded as moral. Kant described two types of commands given by reason: the *hypothetical imperative* which dictates a given course of action to reach a specific end, and the *categorical imperative* which dictates a course of action which must be followed because it is right. The categorical imperative is the basis of morality as stated by Kant: "Act as if the maxim of your action were to become through your will a general natural law." Another view is that of Moore (1971) who held that there is only the duty of producing good. To elaborate, Moore stated that what makes an action right is that such actions produce *more good* than any other action open to the agent. Conflicts of duties are thus resolved by asking, "By what action will the most good be produced?"

The English philosopher, Ross, has attacked what he describes as this "act utilitarian" theory claiming that it is incompatible with our moral beliefs. For example, one can imagine situations in which a utilitarian would decide that most good would be produced by ignoring duties, breaking promises, or swindling a shopkeeper. All of these acts could be committed in the name of utility but all would be considered wrong.

Ross believes that certain duties arise as a result of our special relationships with others. He holds that such special relationships as parent to child, wife to husband, creditor to debtor and the like form the foundation for a prima facie duty which cannot be ignored. "There is nothing arbitrary about these prima facie duties. Each rests on a definite circumstance which cannot seriously be held to be without moral significance."

Throughout this section we have used the term "good" but have not yet provided a definition for it. It is misleading to imply that a precise definition of this term can be supplied for "good" is an exceedingly ambiguous term. Good is often used to mean something that is approved of or something that is desirable. Perry (1964) appears to use good when referring to interest as well as to describe something that is favored.

Definitions of this sort are at best only partially helpful to our present discussion. But since we are referring to good and bad ethical practices we need at least to have a frame of reference for what we are talking about.

In all activities we hold some things to be "good" and others "bad." We favor some actions and disfavor others. Thus good is something which is approved or which is desired by the community. In other senses, "good" may be used to describe food, as "a good dinner," or the weather as in "a good day." We must also note that we will disagree about what is good. Not all people will agree that an action is "good" or that bright sunshine makes a "good" day.

Without further elaboration, the authors hold that some behaviors are "good" and some are "bad;" some actions are favored and some are disfavored. We argue that ethical actions which are helpful to others are *good* while actions which cause harm to others are bad.

With reference to the question posed at the beginning of this chapter, "Can anyone speak clearly of 'right' and 'wrong' actions?" we admit to considerable ambiguity in terminology and recognize sensible disagreement over emotional terms such as "right" and "wrong." However, we maintain that some professional actions of counselors and psychotherapists are helpful to their clients and others are harmful. Such actions are either right or wrong depending upon the effects. Moreover, we maintain that because of their special relationships with clients, counselors have prima facie duties to persons who come to them for professional help. The professional associations have developed some guidelines which can serve as starting places in ethical decision-making. These guidelines or measures must be refined and new ones must be developed by members of the profession, both individually and as a corporate group. Further, there is a considerable amount of research information and professional literature which can provide useful suggestions on how counselors can appropriately assist a variety of client populations.

These points will be elaborated and clarified in the chapters that follow.

SUMMARY

This text deals mainly with ethics and ethical decision-making in the helping professions. Ethics is a topic which, at one time or another, holds considerable interest for everyone. Ethics deals with "right" and "wrong" actions and attempts to understand the complexities of human conduct.

We maintain that some actions are "right" and others "wrong." In the helping professions we argue that actions of professional helpers are "right" if they produce positive results for the persons who seek help. Conversely, actions which have negative effects upon those seeking help are "wrong." Professional association standards, and ethical codes, along with a sizeable body of professional literature, provide some direction for the "right" actions of counselors and psychotherapists.

Because of the special relationships which psychological helpers have with their clients, these professionals have some prima facie duties which are both complex and unique. These duties have considerable moral significance and should be clearly understood by those who attempt to provide psychological assistance to their fellow man.

Chapter Two

ETHICS IN CONTEMPORARY SOCIETY

It is often said that we live in a complex society — in an age of transition or in troubled times. Each generation seems to view its era as different or more troubled than the previous one. In Biblical days religious leaders were much concerned about declining morality, a concern which was apparently quite valid. Few modern accounts of wickedness, lurid as they may be, can equal the stories of sin and depravity among the residents of the ancient cities of Sodom and Gomorrah. Later, Socrates was distressed about the wickedness and indolent behavior of the youth of Athens, and in the colonial era, Cotton Mather wrote extensively on sin and evil in New England. We will shed no new light on the topic of sin in this chapter for that is not our purpose. Rather our purpose is to attempt to bring some clarity to the problem of ethics and morality in modern society. We hope that a discussion of these topics will provide a broader perspective on ethical issues and problems and also will suggest some tentative approaches to problem solving in matters having ethical significance.

In his book, *Man for Himself*, Fromm (1947) points out that Western man has made great strides in understanding and mastering nature and that this achievement would seem to produce comfort and happiness for a large number of people. Technology has enabled mankind to secure the material conditions of a dignified and productive existence, and while many of the goals have not yet been reached, there is little doubt that many problems of the past have been solved.

We may be justifiably proud of our scientific and technical accomplishments. Yet there is considerable evidence that we often feel uneasy and at times bewildered. We work and strive but are dimly aware of a sense of futility with regard to our activities. According to Fromm, while our power over matter grows, we often feel powerless in our individual lives and in society. While creating new and better means for mastering nature, man "has become

14

enmeshed in a network of those means and has lost the vision of the end which alone gives them significance — man himself." While becoming the master of nature, "he has become the slave of the machine which his own hands built." With all of our knowledge about nature, we are ignorant about such fundamental problems as what we are and how we ought to live.

In former times mankind used the ethical norms of the church as a guide to individual behavior. These standards lost some significance during the age of enlightenment where "reason" and "trust your knowledge" became the watchwords for human conduct. The current growing doubt and moral confusion has left us without either reason or relevation. Without these guidelines, Fromm believes that the demands of the state, and enthusiasm for powerful machines, powerful leaders, and material success become the sources for behavioral norms, values, and ethical judgments.

Reisman's (1961) sociological model contains several similar concepts. He suggests that when people freed themselves from a rigid and authoritarian moral code, they sought direction from within and thus became "inner directed." In this system the person observes and internalizes the values of parents at an early formative stage. The individual then develops a personal moral code which guides behavior in the future even when explicit guidelines are not available. Reisman believes that we are now in a new era marked by the development of new moral standards. Such terms as "other-directed" and "mass society" provide a description of today's society. In this society, the individual is greatly influenced by other people and personal values and conduct are a product not of the individual's inner bearings but are introjected from "mass society." Observers such as Reisman and Whyte (1956) argue that in a highly complex environment, individuals are increasingly dependent upon each other but at the same time often find they are in each other's way. Values are based upon productivity, economic status, and the possession of material wealth. In order to get ahead, and perhaps even to survive, the individual must conform to the standards and practices of others.

In his discussion of the "marketplace orientation," Kemp (1967) wrote that a person in contemporary society is constantly reminded that the individual is valued not so much for what s/he thinks or knows, but for what s/he produces. Children learn quite early that they are loved much more if they conform to standards based on success and productivity. Thus, young people have no basis for self-respect; their significance is unrelated to their beliefs, their values, or even to the fact that they are people. Kemp argues that as societies become saturated with technology, people lose their individuality. They become depersonalized, products on the market like the machines they have helped to produce. It is not wisdom or understanding of persons that is considered significant, but the impersonal knowledge of mechanistic naturalism.

While the various "revolutions" in communication, transportation, and industry have brought about greater interdependence among individuals, it is said that people have grown estranged from one another. Family ties have weakened or diminished, parochial beliefs have been challenged, and there are few unifying values to replace them. Simultaneously, greater social mobility leads to concern over status, loss of direction, and problems with identity. There is increased anxiety, depression, and feelings of isolation, and the individual is in constant danger of becoming one of the "lonely crowd."

Some experts question these viewpoints. Grossback and Gardner (1971) cite Bell's (1962) criticism of several views of contemporary society. Bell questions the concept "mass society" and points out that individuals who live in the same environment and do the same things do not necessarily respond in the same way. "Would one say that several hundred or a thousand individuals, who go home alone at night and read the same book, constitute a mass?"

Bell claims that the critics have been fooled by appearances. They see people doing the same things, living in similar houses, driving similar cars, and erroneously conclude that these people think alike. From that conclusion it is then easy to decide that people are alike. What has happened, according to Bell, is that a greater percentage of mankind has become visible than was the case in the past. More people have the means to own cars and houses, and the mobility to be visible. This creates some anxiety in conservative intellectuals who have traditionally referred to the "masses" as the "mindless masses."

In Bell's view the most salient fact about modern life is change. By change he means the striving for material, economic betterment, greater opportunity for the individual and participation by a larger number of people. He fails to see how anyone can be opposed to these trends but concludes that this is the box that some theorists have talked themselves into. Bell identifies the advantage of these values: the right to privacy and a free choice of friends and occupations, status based on achievement rather than assignment, and a plurality of norms and standards rather than the exclusive and monopolistic controls of a dominant group.

Whatever argument one favors, it seems clear that the contemporary individual is faced with several ambiguities as s/he attempts to deal with questions of morality and ethics. Lowe (1976) writes that the present moral situation fails to provide people with a moral focus which tradition or reason once did. As people look to other people for guidance they cannot discover any single authoritative system of morals to which the peer group gives assent. Instead, in a society which has become politically and ideologically open, the person perceives contrasting value orientations which compete for personal allegiance and provide the individual with choices not available in earlier times.

Moral ambiguity can have several negative effects. When values are too unstructured, clinical symptoms can appear. When the moral world seems chaotic, extreme anxiety and frustration may result. Moral indifference and ambiguity can also manifest itself in a general philosophical, ideological, and political dissatisfaction. When one has no guidelines for what is good or bad, right or wrong, life may appear insignificant and it therefore means little what one does with one's life (Lowe, 1976).

Several additional questions implicit in this discussion can now be stated more directly. How can people deal with moral ambiguity? In the absence of generally acceptable moral guidelines how does the individual reach moral and ethical decisions? Dunham (1971) has asked the questions thusly: "How shall a man live his life and build his character in such an environment?" "Can we fare with some decency?"

Counselors and psychotherapists are becoming more aware of the need to deal with these questions as they work with people seeking solutions to problems in daily living. Helping professionals need a clear grasp of some moral and ethical issues in contemporary society if they are to be positive forces in the lives of people they seek to help.

Dunham believes that in the midst of contradictory ethics and in spite of moral indifference, the persons can remain "decent" and ethical. He recognizes that most groups contain some evil but points out that anyone who wishes to accomplish anything cannot avoid involvement with other persons or groups even when others may be immoral. The individual often finds that he or she cannot pursue a career or make a living without interaction with individuals or groups who are corrupt. But, in order to live and to achieve anything socially useful the persons must have some help and cooperation and become involved in organized activity with others. Once this process begins, the temptation inherent in all politics makes itself felt. The person who would not lie, cheat, or cause others harm in his/her own behalf may now be expected to do so for the good of the group or the organization. In return, the group will assist the individual to reach his or her goals. If anything is to be accomplished the person has to be interested in ends. From an interest in ends, it is a short distance to the belief that the ends justify the means.

How then can we behave ethically? Dunham suggests that we can begin by recognizing that there are moral risks in most human activities. But we are obliged morally by never letting the means be lost in the imagined glory of some end.

It is necessary also to place absolute or near absolute limits on our conduct. This means we should be quite clear about the things we will not do. There are some principles that we will adhere to and some rules we will not violate.

It is probable that some necessary acts harm some people. Whenever our achieving a social good involves harm to others we can try to insure that the good confers immediate benefits, so that it will be clear that it has been worth the harm. When, however, the social gain has come out of a struggle to which the mass of people has dedicated itself, the achieved value will be visible enough, though the losers may not see it.

Values and Value Dilemmas

Throughout this text we have made both implicit and explicit references to the impact of values upon individual conduct. In this section we treat the subject more directly while simultaneously calling attention to values in counseling and psychotherapy.

Buhler (1961) states that one cannot go through counseling without dealing with the problems of values, and no one could engage in psychotherapy as therapist without bringing certain convictions and values into the helping process. These convictions may not be specifically communicated to the client but they underlie the therapist's activity; they help determine the goals of therapy.

Peterson (1976), in his succinct discussion of this topic, states: "In a time when the quest for purpose, meaning, and identity is a major concern, the counselor must become aware of and concerned with values in the counseling process."

Some experts describe *value* as that which is *good*. By *good* they mean ethical, so the terms *value* and *ethics* are often equated. We ascribe a somewhat different meaning to the term, however. Values are attitudes, convictions, wishes, and beliefs about how things ought to be. Values are the principles we live by.

Values lie mainly in the realm of ethics and ethical behavior. They have to do with real and fancied choices. Their sphere is all human conduct in which significant alternatives are available. A choice must exist, and we choose one mode of behavior as preferable or better when compared with other alternatives. Values are hierarchically integrated; that is they are related in respect to a greater or lesser degree of desirability. Without choice there would be no occasion for value judgments and decisions. These conditions provide considerable evidence of the influence of values in counseling and psychotherapy.

Some years ago Williams (1956) drew up an interesting list of American values. He describes values as modes of organizing human conduct. According to Williams a dominant value is one that is extensive throughout the system. The first value he lists as characteristic of American society is "achievement and success." Economic prosperity, bigness, and financial rewards are also major values. The next major value orientation is "activity and work," primarily a legacy from our Puritan past. Williams goes on to list "moral orientation," "humanitarianism," "material comfort," "equality," and "freedom" as characteristic American value orientations.

Several years after Williams published his list of values, Snygg (1972) raised questions about economic values and about what he labeled as "the fiction of economic man." He questioned the validity of viewing material wealth and competition as motives of human behavior. Snygg argued that economic gain was not the only motive for work and productivity. He cited prestige, peer approval, and personal satisfaction as equally important factors in human conduct. Snygg recognized competition as a method often used to get more work out of people or better grades out of students. He noted, however, that competition is a relatively ineffective way for having people produce more and suggested that such methods should be abandoned. Snygg believed that our attempts to link values to individual behavior leave many questions unanswered.

In his scholarly work, *The New Mentality*, Cooper (1969) theorizes that the past three decades have witnessed the birth of a new form of ethical consciousness. This new way of viewing man and the world rejects much of the materialistic value system of the past and moves toward a unitary moral sensitivity. Cooper's "new" mentality with a changed system of values has evolved to a higher ethical sensitivity than ever before, and the direction upward is "measurably increasing from year to year." The new mentality is a "unique ethical cast of mind" that is positive, loving, and humanistic.

Cooper describes some of the value conflicts between the new generation and the old and points out that the youth movements of the 1960s led to a reappraisal of our basic value structure. He believes that some of the pessimistic attitudes and hedonist conduct of the 1960s may have had a negative effect; however, in some cases these practices caused us to analyze our own attitudes and behaviors and in those instances the effects were positive.

The task of value analysis is quite difficult. This is not an area of "facts" or "truths" derived from methodical research, but rather an area of differing views and positions. Part of the difficulty lies in the complexity of contemporary society and in the changing nature of Western culture: A casual examination of the great diversity in this country, ranging from Wall Street brokers to share croppers in Louisiana, suggests the tentativeness of any generalizations we might make. Further, within the same region and time span, various individuals and groups hold different views on life styles and on such topics as freedom, democracy, honesty, and morality. Philosophers, social scientists, and popular writers do not always agree on the essential characteristics of contemporary values. Consider, for example, the varying interpretations and reactions to such topics as government snooping, abuse of power, and bribery of elected officials. Some social analysts view corruption of public officials and dishonesty in business as a manifestation of general moral deterioration while others maintain that the crimes of a few scoundrels have only indirect relevance to the values and moral fiber of the nation. Analysts do not agree because they read the facts differently, they approach the problem from different perspectives, and because their values are different.

We are persuaded, however, that some values are clearly visible. There is little doubt that we are a production-oriented society: We idealize technology, and we value achievement and success. We admire those who can get things done and we respect one who is successful. We covet material possessions and we like money — generally, the more we have, the more we like it. But there are other important values in this society. For example, some of the ideals upon which our political structure was built — freedom, justice, and equality — are still quite visible. Consider, for example, the political and social changes of the past two decades. Most of these have, or will have eventually, the effects of providing more opportunity and more freedom for people. Or, observe the beginnings of government reform resulting from Watergate and other political chicanery. These reforms are the result of public outrage over dishonesty and immorality among elected officials. One can argue of course that politicians are not more ethical than before Watergate or the General Services Administration swindle, only more afraid of being exposed. But these examples do illustrate that a concern for basic ethical principles is present in much of our society (Van Hoose and Kottler, 1977).

SUMMARY

This chapter describes some of the moral ambiguities of contemporary society. In a world trembling with change traditional standards and guidelines for moral conduct lose much of their significance. Contrasting value orientations and the availability of an array of choices make it difficult for the individual to find a focus for ethical decision-making.

In such an environment, how can a person discover some ethical principles which will give direction to individual conduct? In a climate of ethical confusion can one behave ethically? The authors take the position that it is possible for the individual to deal successfully with the ethical problems of modern society. In order to do so, however, the person must first analyze his or her behavior and then set some guidelines for individual conduct.

Value orientations have a significant influence upon individual conduct. The task of value analysis is quite complex; however, some values which permeate contemporary society are clearly identifiable. Values lie primarily within the realm of ethics and ethical conduct. It is not likely that one can be an effective counselor without dealing with value problems.

Chapter Three

PERSPECTIVES ON ETHICAL THEORY

One of the purposes of this chapter is to illustrate the relationship between ethical theory and ethical practice, and to identify the connection between philosophical principles and the practice of counseling and psychotherapy. For many counseling practitioners, ethical philosophy may seem quite remote from their everyday professional activities. It is our hope to dispel this belief by illustrating how the philosophical formulations of others quite often illuminate our own ethical conduct.

Often one knows what actions *ought* to or *should* be done, but is not aware of the reasons why they *ought* to or *should* be done. Under normal circumstances, this difficulty poses no real dilemma for the individual. It is only when we face unfamiliar situations or problems for which there are no clearly defined solutions that we must look to some higher level of inquiry rather than simple reliance on past experiences to guide our actions. Abelson and Friquegnon (1975) summarize it well when they state:

> "Ethical philosopy is the effort to resolve conflicts rationally, when our automatic responses and implicit rules of action collide with contrary responses and rules. When opposition from others or from our own conscience makes us aware of arguments against our actions and policies, it becomes necessary for us to provide reasons for them, and thus to engage in philosophical discussion."

It is in this context that ethical formulations from three philosophical positions will be presented. Hedonism, self-actualization, and moral developmentalism will be examined because of their unique relevance and singular contributions to the theoretical development of counseling.

What is ethical theory?

For centuries scholars have struggled with what is meant by the concept of ethics. It has come to mean many different things to many different writers. G.E. Moore (1971) summarizes the immense amount of disagreement on the subject matter of ethical philosophy in his book, *Ethics*. Following Moore's definition, ethics is that which deals with the question of what is good or bad, right or wrong in human conduct. Applying this directly to counseling, Van Hoose and Kottler (1977) suggest that the study of ethics may be described as a systematic way in which a counselor can make moral decisions based upon an underlying philosophy that is consistent with his or her beliefs and congruent with institutional, societal and professional policies.

Theory is commonly defined as a systematic way of organizing a body of knowledge in order to *understand*, *explain*, and *predict*. However, the use of the word *theory* in ethics should not be confused with its use in science, for there is quite a difference. Our definition for theory, then, may require some slight modification when we speak of ethics. Ethical theory does not help us understand what is, was, or will be the case as scientific theory does. It is concerned with what ought to be the case or what one ought to do. It is in this sense that scientific theory is descriptive or factual and ethical theory is normative. That is, ethical theory is concerned with the principles or norms that ought to govern one's conduct. Abelson and Friquegnon (1975) aptly convey this distinction and illuminate the function of ethical theory:

> "Science gives us information about the world, while ethics gives us rules and standards for changing the world to fit our requirements. A scientific theory provides a hypothesis for predicting what will happen, while an ethical theory provides a standard for making things happen."

In addition, ethical theory focuses on the general issues of human conduct — those questions that are likely to be dealt with repeatedly and to be applicable to all persons. Why is it better to take a particular course of action rather than another one? As Brandt (1961) suggests, ethical theories are concerned with which general ethical principles are true or valid or defensible. As such, they are not concerned with specific questions about specific situations. However, as Brandt and other ethical philosophers note, general ethical principles are highly relevant to the solution of specific ethical dilemmas. It is this very premise upon which this chapter on ethical theory is predicated: Ethical theory can provide an avenue from which to help in the reasoning of specific ethical dilemmas that counselors may face in their day-to-day professional practice.

The Counselor as an Ethical Philosopher

All individuals, counselors being no exception, function on the basis of their own idiosyncratic value system. This value system, which defines what is important to the individual, what priorities exist for him or her, and what is seen as good or bad, right or wrong, is shaped by a myriad of factors — training, past experiences, education, parental and peer influence, etc. All these factors combine in complex fashion to form the individual's value system. This individual value system is not a constant and static state of affairs. It is continually changing, being modified and revised as the development of the individual occurs. For counselors this changing value system is even more critical because of the tremendous influence they exert over the people they serve. Benjamin (1974) addresses this two-way dialogue between value systems most appropriately:

> "Our clients in the helping interview do not leave our values unchallenged. By examining their own, they may be challenging ours. While insisting that we define for them what is right and wrong, they may be groping for their own ethical standards."

Since values and ethical beliefs are so inherently a *part* of the subject matter of counseling, it is quite necessary that the personal value and ethical system of the counselor be continuously monitored, evaluated, reflected upon, and revised. It is in the examination of our own system that understanding of why we do what we do becomes apparent. However, the fact remains that each individual possesses a unique, personal code of ethical beliefs that, to a large extent, governs his or her conduct. It is in this regard that each therapist is his or her own ethical philosopher. To the degree that consistency of belief from situation to situation, and insight and understanding are present, the counselor will be better served by his or her own ethical philosophy.

It should not be construed, however, that there exists a totally different ethical philosophy for every separate individual. Common elements consistent with societal norms and expectations from social, religious, and professional groups (see the Appendix for the expectations of the American Personnel and Guidance Association and the American Psychological Association in their standards of ethical conduct) are quite apparent and exert considerable influence on what individuals come to espouse as their own personal ethical philosophy. The ethical philosophies presented later in this chapter similarly have influenced the thinking of counselors and can continue to provide understanding and awareness of the ethical inquiry necessary for professional development.

Three Approaches to Ethics

Three theoretical approaches to ethics (hedonism, self-actualization, and moral developmentalism) have been selected for inquiry because of their direct relevance to the contemporary ethical thinking of counseling practitioners. While the list of ethical philosophies and approaches spans centuries and encompasses a multitude of differences of opinion, both within and across the varying schools of thought, it is hoped that these three approaches will provide insight into the basic question of what is ethical in human conduct. Considering that such contemporary ethical dilemmas as terrorism, abortion, suicide, genetic research, test-tube babies, euthanasia, and Watergate have aroused the ethical awareness of society, the posing of this basic question seems more justifiable than ever before. Apart from the larger ethical dilemmas facing society, practicing counselors are now faced with ethical dilemmas involving malpractice, negligence. and accountability. Perhaps an awareness of the basic ideas of previous writers will help the reader to become more aware of his or her own ethical and moral posture. The reader interested in pursuing ethical theory should consult the bibliography appearing in this text for further resources.

Hedonism. The hedonistic approach, espoused primarily by the utilitarian philosophies of Jeremy Bentham, John Stuart Mill, Henry Sidgwick and G.E. Moore, are perhaps best summarized by the maxim that the best condition is one in which the balance of pleasure over pain is the greater. This basic approach to ethics, first expounded by Francis Hutcheson in 1725, owes its initial development to the ancient Greek philosopher Epicurus (342 B. C. - 270 B. C.) who saw pleasure as the prime good. The industrial revolution, occurring in Great Britain during the eighteenth century, provided much of the socio-economic impetus for the ethical reasoning underlying the utilitarian philosophy (Russell, 1959).

While a diverse range of ideas comprises the hedonist orientation, the approach is one of a few which attempts to deduce universal moral principles for relatively few basic tenets. Admittedly this somewhat reductionistic and common sense approach to human conduct has had considerable impact upon our understanding of human behavior. The utilitarian idea that man is guided by the pursuit of pleasure and the avoidance of pain has been a theoretical cornerstone of the behavioral approaches to psychology and counseling. Jeremy Bentham (1748-1832) was the first of the utilitarian philosophers. Ethics for him was primarily a basis for examining the legal ways of promoting the best possible state of affairs for society. Bentham was greatly involved in social and religious reform and was considered quite a radical in England. Russell (1959) notes that while Bentham had started with views that were not notably radical, he became, in later life, an aggressive atheist. In fact he was the leader of a group of men known as the Philosophical Radicals.

Briefly, he believed that individuals try to attain the greatest possible happiness or pleasure. In doing so, he felt, that no one should impede this pursuit for others. By this belief, the greatest good is achieved for the greatest number.

The ideal of the greatest good for the greatest number, in many ways, is the unifying ethical principle among the many differences of the utilitarians. Thus, what one ought to do is guided by the pursuit of pleasure and the avoidance of pain for oneself as well as for others.

Bentham's version of utilitarianism is philosophically simpler than other utilitarian theorists. His proposal for deciding the rightness of an action is not totally unlike many of the problem solving approaches to counseling where alternatives are advanced and weighed against the possible consequences of each before a decision based upon possible outcomes is derived. The following is Bentham's utilitarian approach to ethical problem solving, written in 1789:

> "Sum up all the values of all the pleasures on the one side, and those of all the pains on the other. The balance, if it be on the side of pleasure, will give the good tendency of the act upon the whole, with respect to the interests of that individual person; if on the side of pain, the bad tendency of it upon the whole."

Bentham's contribution to our contemporary ethical thinking seems to lie in this problem solving approach to what one ought to do, that is, weighing the pleasure against the pain in deciding the ethical course of action.

While Bentham was the leader of the Philosophical Radicals, the force behind the movement was John Stuart Mill (1806-1873). Like his contemporary Bentham, and Epicurus centuries before him, Mill, in his classic work, *Utilitarianism*, first published in 1863, tried to establish that pleasure is the only thing instrinsically worthwhile of greater relevance. Mill attempted to carry the utilitarian approach even further by addressing the question, "Which acts are right or wrong?" He proposed that an act is right if, and only if, it will, or probably will, or tends to, produce at least as much good as any other action a person might have also performed.

Mill regarded certain pleasures as qualitatively better than others. "It may be objected that many who are capable of higher pleasures, occasionally, under the influence of temptation, postpone them to the lower. Men often, from infirmity of character, make their election for the nearer good, though they know it to be less valuable" (Mill, 1961).

Mill has been criticized (Russell, 1969) for his lack of precision in explaining the differentiation between qualitatively better pleasures and mere difference in quantity. However, he did address one criticism of utilitarian ethical philosophy which has direct practical implications for the individual faced with an ethical question. That is, the individual may not have sufficient time before an act to calculate its relative utility and to estimate its consequences or determine its potential for producing pleasure. Certainly the ethical decision-making process suggested by Bentham would require time for reflective thought. Presumably Mill believed this to be one justification for the presence of a code of ethics upon which one's actions could be guided. However, he skeptically noted that there has been sufficient time in the whole duration of the human species to have developed such a code.

Henry Sidgwick (1838-1900) developed an approach to utilitarian ethics based upon reason and rationality. He took exception to Bentham's simplistic ethical tenet of the greatest happiness by proclaiming that Bentham's logic though not quite a tautology could hardly serve as the fundamental principle of a moral system.

He spoke of ethical actions being judged as reasonable and rational and, therefore, the ultimate ends should be prescribed by reason. "For we commonly think that wrong conduct is essentially irrational, and can be shown to be so by argument; and though we do not conceive that it is by reason alone that men are influenced to act rightly, we still hold that appeals to the reason are an essential part of all moral persuasion" (Sidgwick, 1961).

As Jones, Sontag, Beckner, and Fogelin (1969) note, Sidgwick identified three basic approaches from his study of the history of ethical theory: (a) *Egoistic hedonism* — if it is pleasurable to the individual, it should be done; (b) *Universalistic hedonism* — what is best for everyone involved should be done with unselfish benevolence; and (c) *Institutionalism* — actions based upon absolute moral truths without concern for consequences should be done.

Sidgwick argued for the existence of these absolute moral truths but felt that they were too abstract and needed to be explicated. It was in this effort that he felt utilitarianism could make its best contribution. We shall see later in this chapter, when we discuss the work of Lawrence Kohlberg on moral development, the refinement of many of Sidgwick's earlier notions for the role of reasoning in moral and ethical judgment. G. E. Moore (1873 - 1958),

the most contemporary utilitarian, can be credited with illuminating the study of ethical theory with his first and classic work,
Principa Ethica.   In it he discussed the basic principles of ethical
reasoning citing two questions as the key to the study of ethics:
What kind of things are intrinsically good? What kind of actions
ought we to perform?

To examine the question of what is good, Moore (1971), following Sidgwick's reasoning, suggested that "good" is a simple, indefin-
able property and any attempt to define it is impossible.

> "Everyone does, in fact, understand the question 'Is this good?'
> When he thinks of it, his state of mind is different from what it would be,
> were he asked 'Is this pleasant?' . . . . . It has distinct meaning for him,
> even though he may not recognize in what respect it is distinct. . . . . . But
> for correct ethical reasoning, it is extremely important that he should be-
> come aware of this fact; and, as soon as the nature of the problem is
> clearly understood, there should be little difficulty in advancing so far
> in analysis."

In much the same way as his predecessor, John Stuart Mill,
Moore (1969) explained the difference between right and wrong.
He stated that an action is right whenever the individual could not,
even if he or she had chosen, have done any other action instead,
which could have caused more pleasure than the action selected.

Thus, the common philosophical thread of the hedonist position — the pursuit of pleasure (the right) over pain (the wrong) at
no other's expense — translates into the utilitarian axiom of the
greatest good for the greatest number. For the practicing counselor,
this approach to ethical reasoning suggests reflection on the positive
and negative consequences of given actions and their potential impact upon all parties involved before courses of action are selected.
Bentham's mid-eighteenth century approach to ethical decision
making holds up rather well when weighed against counseling's contemporary problem-solving strategies (e. g., Carkhuff, 1973; Gelatt,
1962; Krumboltz & Thoresen, 1976; Tolbert, 1974).

Self-actualization. The advocates of the self-actualization approach to human conduct view man as innately good with the ability
toward positive growth and development. This basic belief has seen
renewed interest with the rise of the humanist movement in philosophy, psychology and counseling during the later part of this century.
The optimistic view that individuals are good and creative possessing
an innate potential to strive toward ethically appropriate conduct
is highlighted by this approaches' emphases on human freedom and
dignity, trust, and the limitless potential for growth.

Proponents making singular contributions to self-actualization are numerous and span centuries of thought. The formulations of Aristotle, Erich Fromm, Abraham Maslow, Rollo May, and Carl Rogers will be presented in this section.

Aristotle (384 B.C.–323 B.C.) perhaps one of the greatest minds in the history of civilization, can probably be credited with providing the philosophical foundation for contemporary self-actualization theories. His *Nicomachean Ethics* is one of the great classics in ethical theory. Aristotle believed that every action by individuals is directed at some good and, therefore, the good is thought to be that to which all things aim (Allan, 1970; Rackham, 1952).

Aristotle believed the absolute good could be pursued by the attainment of happiness by means of virtue. Virtue is seen as a mean between extremes of character. The absolute good is not achieved by everyone to the same extent, but it is nonetheless the highest goal man can attain. As we shall see, this notion will serve centuries later as a basic element for the modern theories of self-actualization. For Aristotle, virtues (e.g., courage, composure and justice) are those which motivate ethical human conduct. His ultimate conclusion stated that rational activity is the good, not only reflection on good but practical action consistent with rational principles. Aristotle's ethical beliefs adapted from Brandt (1961) can be summarized as follows:

- The good is what is desired for itself.
- The subject matter of ethics is so complex that simple generalizations are not possible.
- The good is happiness in the sense of well-being or satisfaction, but individuals will differ greatly in their conception of it.
- Man is distinctive from all other things by his reason; therefore happiness is the exercise of reason in living.
- Happiness requires an entire life time; moral excellence is the result of practice in acting rightly.

Most importantly to later ethical thought, Aristotle proclaimed that an act does not demonstrate more excellence merely by being right; its motivation must be moral. That is to say, the individual must know what s/he is doing; it must not be an accidental or random effort. The principle of the awareness of the underlying rationale for rightness would later serve as a basic formulation of several modern approaches to moral and ethical reasoning – e. g., Kohlberg's moral development theory and Van Hoose and Paradise's stages of ethical judgment.

Aristotle's contributions are so vast that it is quite beyond the scope of this chapter to adequately examine them. Interested readers are encouraged to pursue the work of Aristotle not only for its timeless insights, but also for its direct relevance to the fields of psychology, philosophy and education.

Erich Fromm (1947), the neopsychoanalyst, has demonstrated in his study of humanist ethics, the role of psychology in understanding human conduct. Focusing on the importance of reason and the individuality of man, he notes:

> "Man is capable of discerning and making value judgments as valid as all other judgments derived from reason. The great tradition of humanistic ethical thought has laid the foundation for value systems based on man's autonomy and reason."

Thus, Fromm believes the resources for ethical conduct reside in man's human nature. He sees the function of ethical systems as that of sustaining life for the society. He believes the human conscience, which he describes as the internalized reaction of the total personality in its capacity to be human, to be the ultimate source of moral and ethical regulation. "Conscience judges our functioning as human beings; it is knowledge within oneself, knowledge of our respective success or failure in the act of living."

Why then has the notion of conscience been so ineffective in the moral and ethical regulation of conduct? Fromm provides a simple answer, stating that man's refusal to listen, and even more importantly, the ignorance of knowing how to listen, results in ethical and moral crises for the individual.

Fromm has faith in man's power to discern good from bad, suggesting that if there is to be confidence in values, man must know himself and the capacity of his nature for goodness.

Fromm contrasted what he termed authoritarian ethics, some external power figure imposing laws and rules, with humanistic ethics, based on the requirements of man's human nature. Reflecting the self-actualization approaches, Fromm believes that failure to develop potentials and fullness is the "capital crime" of humanistic ethics. This basic belief in man's potential and striving for goodness is also reflected in other prominent theorists with humanist orientations (e. g., Adler, 1954; Jung, 1964; Rogers, 1961).

Abraham Maslow (1908 - 1970) was a pioneer and major contributor to what has been referred to as "the third force" in psychology – the humanist movement. In reaction to the two major psychology orientations of that time, psychoanalysis and behaviorism, Maslow began to develop much of what is presently known as humanistic psychology.

Maslow (1955) questioned the traditional hedonist assumption that pleasure and pain were the major sources of motivation for man. Instead he proposed that man's striving for growth, for happiness and satisfaction be examined. Maslow terms the person who achieves these ends, self-actualizing. It is these individuals who have a clear notion between ends and means. Means are easily interchanged, but ends tend to be permanent. Unlike the average person, the self-actualizing individual does not show confusion and conflicting beliefs and can be definitely described, according to Maslow, as ethical in conduct.

Maslow believed that values are intrinsically developed from within, chosen by the person. Therapy and counseling, one could argue, following Maslow's theoretical position, are a search for values — an effort where the individual attempts to develop to his/her fullest functioning: self-actualization.

Much of the impetus for the self-actualizing theories lies with the influence of the existentialist philosophy developed in Germany and France during the early twentieth century, exemplified by the writings of such prominent philosophers and theologians as Karl Jaspers, Soren Kierkegaard, Martin Heidegger, Paul Tillich, and Jean-Paul Sartre. While these individuals represent considerable divergence in their emphases, their main argument has been that rationalism and empiricism as a philosophy are unable to provide a viable account of the meaning of human existence. The existential influence on counseling and psychotherapy is best illustrated by the works of May (1953, 1967), Rogers (1951, 1961), and Arbuckle (1965). The ideas of May and Rogers will be examined.

Rollo May, the most eloquent spokesman for the existential position, has written much in the area of counseling and psychotherapy. Many of his ideas are directly related to basic ethical questions underlying the helping profession.

May (1967) believes that all problems and emotional disturbances are related to the primary ethical question, "How shall I live my life?" Given this assumption, the role of the counselor becomes one of facilitating moral adjustment. Within this process is the undeniable right of the client to develop his or her own moral system. Thus, the client has the capacity and potential to make decisions and develop a moral system.

Perhaps no other exponent of the humanist position has had more impact upon the counseling profession than Carl Rogers. Since Rogers' first work, *Counseling and Psychotherapy*, in 1942, his client-centered approach to counseling has become a landmark for all those in the field. Rogers (1951) like others from this orientation believes in the inherent tendency of the individual for growth and actualization. Rogers (1961) agrees with Maslow that one of the most basic principles of human nature is that man's motivations and tendencies are positive. According to Rogers, man is essentially forward-looking, sensitively humane, and good.

Rogers (1972) in his approach to values recommends listening to oneself. A person should let his or her experiences suggest meaning rather than force meaning upon the experiences. If allowed to develop to full potential, the individual has a set of values, moral standards, and ethical principles to guide conduct. The principles are one's own and an integral part of one's existence.

The self-actualization approaches presented in this discussion are all in agreement that the individual has the capacity to make ethical decisions that are good and right and to assume the responsibility for the appropriateness of these decisions as they affect human conduct. The moral developmentalists also support this basic assumption.

Moral Developmentalism. The moral developmentalist approach represents an integration of psychology and child development. It has been derived mainly from scientific research and case history observation rather than reliance on philosophic reflection. However, Kohlberg (1971) a leading proponent, suggests that the concept of morality must be considered as a philosophical rather than a behavioral concept. Thus, moral developmentalism reflects an inter-disciplinary approach to the study of ethics and morals.

Common to the various moral development positions is the belief that morality is not a collection of positive virtues such as loyalty, honesty, and generosity but rather a view of justice, maturing as a function of the development and experience of the individual. According to Kohlberg (1971) the most essential structure of morality is the principle of justice based upon the distribution of rights regulated by concepts of equality and reciprocity.

"There is only one principled basis for resolving claims: justice or equality, treat every man's claim impartially regardless of the man. A moral principle is not only a rule of action but reason for action" (Kohlberg, 1970).

Moral and ethical behavior is viewed within the context of a series of stages in reasoning and thinking through which all individuals pass in their development. Other common assumptions of the developmentalist approach include:

(a) The basic motivation for morality is a generalized motivation for self-esteem, competence, acceptance, or self-realization rather than anxiety or fear reduction.

(b) Aspects of moral development are culturally universal.

(c) Basic moral norms and principles are structures arising through social interaction experiences rather than the internalization of external rules and codes.

(d) Some sense of age-related sequential reorganizations is found in the development of moral attitudes.

John Dewey (1859-1952), following some of the early writings of J. M. Baldwin (1906), William McDougall (1908), and Leonard Hobhouse (1906), can be credited with the initial evolvement of the developmental approach to morality and ethics. Dewey (1964) postulated three levels of moral development:

(a) *Premoral or preconventional*: behaviors motivated by biological and social impulses.

(b) *Conventional*: the standards of the group are accepted by the individual with little critical reflection.

(c) *Autonomous*: conduct is guided by the individual reasoning for himself what is good; group standards are not accepted without sufficient reflection.

While Dewey's approach to moral development was theoretical, it was not until the classic work of Jean Piaget, the renowned Swiss psychologist and epistemologist, that an empirically based stage theory of moral development was advanced. Piaget, (1926, 1965) through his ingenious and creative approach of interviewing and observing countless numbers of children advanced the following stages of moral development:

(a) *Premoral*: no sense of obligation to rules.

(b) *Heteronomous*: obedience to rules based upon submission to external authorities.

(c) *Autonomous*: development of personally meaningful moral codes based upon reciprocity, i. e., mutual respect for the other's point of view.

Piaget (1965) concludes that all morality consists of a system of rules and that the essence of all morality lies in the respect which the individual acquires for these rules. By observing the "marble playing" behavior of children, Piaget makes the clear distinction between the consciousness and the practice of ethics. The practice of rules is the way children of different ages effectively apply the rules; the consciousness of rules deals with the ideas that children of differing ages form about the character or nature of the rules, that is, whether the rules are sacred or subject to their own choice. Thus, Piaget, just as Sidgwick before him, focused his attention on the reasoning underlying moral and ethical judgments.

Much of the controversy in the field of moral development has centered around the issue of relative or absolute morality. In contemporary psychological terminology this is defined as situationally specific versus universal ethical or moral behavior. Considerable justification for situationally specific moral behavior over the moral developmentalist position is due in great part to the classic experimental work of Hartshorne and May (1928, 1930).

Hartshorne and May studied the behavior of approximately 11,000 children who were given the opportunity to lie, cheat, or steal in activities associated with school, home and athletic interactions. They found that the inconsistency of children's moral behavior was remarkable. For example, it was impossible to predict whether a child who cheated on an arithmetic test would cheat in other situations. They also found that moral behavior did not correlate with moral knowledge. Children who had perfect Sunday school attendance cheated more than those who had never attended a church school. The researchers concluded that there were no honest or dishonest people and that individuals who cheat in one situation will not necessarily cheat in another. Directly related to the issue of ethics, they concluded that verbalizations about what people believe is ethical have little to do with the way they act. These sobering conclusions on the moral and ethical character of man were summarized by May (1978): "Behavior happens to be determined more by the situation in which you are placed than it is by some internal thing called honesty."

Hartshorne and Mays' pioneering results cast some doubts on the stage theories of the moral developmentalists and served as the basis for the social learning (situation specific) approach to morality. For a comprehensive review of the research related to the social learning position, see Mischel and Mischel (1976).

In defense of the moral developmentalist position, it should be noted that some years later Burton (1963) reanalyzed the original Hartshorne and May data with modern statistical methods to reconsider the notion of situationally specific morality. He found some consistency of moral behavior across situations. Similarly other research has later confirmed this moral consistency (Heilman, Hodgson & Hornstein, 1972; Hetherington & Feldman, 1964; Nelson, Grinder & Mutterer, 1969, Sears, Rau & Alpert, 1965).

Commenting upon the merits of the controversy between the moral developmental and social learning positions, Van Hoose and Kottler (1977) note that the dichotomy is an oversimplification which has obscured the real issues and created unnecessary theoretical conflicts. They note that Hartshorne and May were concerned with whether people violate ethical principles and under what circumstances, while the moral developmentalists were concerned with the *reasoning* underlying moral judgments. Seen from this perspective, the elements from one approach do not necessarily contraindicate the elements from the other. Van Hoose and Kottler conclude that although moral behavior can be seen as situation specific relative to circumstances involved, moral reasoning can be viewed as composed of invariant developmental stages that remain absolute across cultures and individuals.

Perhaps no other individual has added more to the theoretical and empirical support for the moral developmentalist position than Lawrence Kohlberg. In 1955 he began to redefine and validate the Dewey-Piaget stages of moral development. His six major stages grouped into three levels are presented in Table 1.

Kohlberg's (1975) basic assumptions for this developmental position include the following:

(a) The stages are organized systems of thought.

(b) Individuals are consistent in the levels of moral reasoning.

(c) The stages form an *invariant* sequence of development with movement always being forward.

(d) Moral reasoning at a higher stage includes within it lower stage reasoning with tendency on the part of the individual to prefer the highest stage available.

Based upon a considerable body of validating research over the years, Kohlberg (1976) concludes:

> "To act in a morally high way requires a high stage of moral reasoning. One cannot follow moral principles if one does not understand or believe in them. One can, however, reason in such terms and not live up to them. A variety of factors determines whether a particular person will live up to his stage of moral reasoning in a particular situation, though moral stage is a good predictor of action in various experimental and naturalistic settings."

Kohlberg (1976) and his associates have advanced the validity of the developmentalist position on the universality of basic moral beliefs with a variety of cross cultural (Canada, Britain, Israel, Taiwan, Honduras, India) and longitudinal studies. Additionally, they have provided an instructional framework for moral education. Suggesting that teachers view the child as possessing an organized system of moral reasoning, Kohlberg advocates that educators expose children to higher levels of moral and ethical reasoning. He argues and research has verified (Blatt & Kohlberg, in press; Rest, Turiel & Kohlberg, 1969; Turiel, 1966) that exposure to the next higher stage of moral reasoning can increase the development of higher levels of moral reasoning.

Table 1: KOHLBERG'S STAGES OF MORAL DEVELOPMENT*

Level One: PRECONVENTIONAL

Stage I	Heteronomous morality	Avoidance of punishment, superior power of authority.	Egocentric viewpoint, does not recognize interests of others.
Stage II	Instrumental purpose	Follow rules only to meet someone's immediate interest.	Concrete individualistic viewpoint; rightness is relative to one's own pursuit in a concrete sense.

Level Two: CONVENTIONAL

Stage III	Mutual interpersonal expectations	Morality of maintaining good relations, approval of others.	Expectations take primacy over individual interests; good boy – nice girl orientation.
Stage IV	Social systems, law and order	Orientation toward maintenance of the social order.	The social system defines right and wrong.

Level Three: POST CONVENTIONAL

Stage V	Social contract, utilitarian orientation	Right action defined by general individual rights and relative to personal values.	Greatest good for greatest number; consideration of conflict between moral and legal viewpoints.
Stage VI	Universal ethical principles	Follows self-chosen ethical principles of justice and equality.	Universal principles outweigh law or social norms.

* Adapted from L. Kohlberg (1976).

Both Kohlberg and Piaget agree that moral development, like cognitive development, is a function of maturation within the context of age-related experience. Similar to the self-actualization theorists, they believe in the innate goodness of the individual, that is, if the individual is allowed to develop naturally, he or she will become an ethical being.

The Stages of Ethical Behavior

The present writers, strongly influenced by the work of Piaget and Kohlberg, conceptualized the ethical behavior of counselors along a developmental continuum (Van Hoose, 1971; Paradise, 1976; Van Hoose & Paradise, 1977). It was proposed that the ethical orientation of counselors, that is, the rationale underlying individual ethical decision-making, could be viewed from a model of five, qualitatively different stages of ethical reasoning. These ethical orientations are presented in Table 2.

Within this theoretical framework, the following formulations were proposed:

(a) Most counselors do not function solely at one given stage, variations being a function of situation, training, and other related variables.

(b) The proposed ethical orientations not only describe qualitatively discrete stages, but reflect an underlying continuum of ethical reasoning from which the basis of ethical judgments are made. Thus, the conclusion that certain ethical judgments are more adequate, appropriate, or correct appears to be a safe assumption.

(c) The basis for the counselors's judgment, when faced with an ethical dilemma, is characterized in terms of the counselor's dominant stage of ethical orientation.

(d) The stages of ethical orientation are continuous and overlapping, suggestive of movement towards higher levels of ethical reasoning.

(e) Movement in ethical judgment, the reasoning process underlying ethical decision-making, is forward and irreversible, while ethical action, overt behavior associated with an ethical dilemma, need not be forward and is reversible. That is, one may reason at a high level, but one's behavior may reflect a much lower level. One cannot reason at a higher level than his/her subsequent behavior reflects.

(f) Situational influences may produce discrepancies between levels of reasoning and action such that these discrepancies could generate ethical conflict. That is, whenever a person's action is reflective of a lower stage than his or her reasoning, internal ethical conduct is likely to ensue.

Table 2: THE STAGES OF ETHICAL ORIENTATION

STAGE I

Punishment Orientation

Counselor decisions, suggestions, and courses of action are based on a strict adherence to prevailing rules and standards; i. e., one must be punished for bad behavior and rewarded for good behavior. The primary concern is the strict attention to the physical consequences of the behavior.

STAGE II

Institutional Orientation

Counselor decisions, suggestions, and courses of action are based on a strict adherence to the rules and policies of the institution or agency. The correct posture is based upon the expectations of higher authorities.

STAGE III

Societal Orientation

The maintenance of standards, approval of others, and the laws of society and the general public characterize this stage of ethical behavior. The concern is for duty and societal welfare.

STAGE IV

Individual Orientation

The primary concern of the counselor is for the needs of the individual while avoiding the violation of laws and the rights of others. Concern for law and societal welfare is recognized, but is secondary to the needs of the individual.

STAGE V

Principle or Conscience Orientation

Concern for the individual is primary with little regard for the legal, professional, or societal consequences. What is right, in accord with self-chosen principles of conscience and internal ethical formulations, determines counselor behavior.

Examining Table 2, it can be seen that at *Stage I*, the ethical orientation is exclusively dependent upon external rationale. Counselor functioning at this stage is governed by the sanctions and physical consequences of the behavior involved. When faced with an ethical dilemma, reasoning becomes fundamental and absolute. At *Stage II*, the rules and policies of the institution or agency with which one is associated provide the ethical decision making rationale. There is little room for conflict with the expectations of higher authorities. Following orders, "the book" provides the rationale for ethical decision-making.

At *Stage III*, reasoning is based upon general societal welfare. Judgment is derived from the norms and laws set by society. When the individual and society are in conflict, the individual is secondary to society.

Stage IV reflects judgment based upon what is best for the individual. Concern is for the needs of the individual, though the needs of society are not overlooked. The counselor functioning at this stage considers the individual his/her primary concern and the societal context as secondary. At this stage, the reasoning underlying ethical judgments is internally oriented in contrast to the preceding stages where guidelines and expectations were external in their origin.

Stage V represents the highest level of ethical orientation. It is here that the individual is primary with little concern for legal and societal consequences. Right is defined by individual decisions of conscience and justice consistent with one's own defined internal ethical code. The counselor operating under this orientation reflects upon his or her principles of ethics and morality without regard to external pressures, consequences or situational factors.

To assess the stages of ethical orientation, *The Ethical Judgment Scale* (Van Hoose & Goldman, 1971; Van Hoose & Paradise, 1979) was developed. The scale (see page 113) containing twenty-five hypothetical ethical dilemmas that may confront a counselor in his or her work, has been shown in previous studies to be useful in both validating the theoretical formulations which have been proposed and providing an instructional framework for examining and increasing the ethical awareness of counselors (Paradise, 1978).

SUMMARY

In this chapter we have presented in historical perspective three theoretical approaches to ethics: hedonism, self-actualization and moral developmentalism. Hedonism, based on the pursuit of pleasure and avoidance of pain, professes the utilitarian ethical principle of the greatest good for the greatest number. The self-actualization approach views the individual as innately good with the capacity for growth and development toward moral and ethically appropriate behavior. The moral developmentalist approach focuses upon the reasoning underlying the moral and ethical judgments of the individual. The approach is characterized by various qualitatively different stages of reasoning that the individual progresses through as a function of maturation and age-related experience.

Additionally, a developmental approach to the ethical judgment of counselors was presented. It conceptualized five qualitatively different stages of ethical orientation which reflect the underlying rationale used by counselors when faced with ethical dilemmas.

From the discussion in this chapter, it can be seen that no definitive system of morality or ethical behavior is commonly accepted by everyone. Just as there are scores of counseling theories with considerable implications for the practitioner, there are also many existing approaches to morality. In all probability, there exists a different system of morality for each practitioner based upon his or her personality, belief system, values, and expectations.

It is quite unlikely that anyone will be in total or exact agreement with any of the theorists previously discussed. However, the theorists' positions have been greatly consolidated and simplified in order to stimulate reflection upon one's own ethical orientation and the factors that may contribute to it. Perhaps some of the formulations of these theorists can help the reader to further examine his or her personal system of ethics.

Chapter Four

RESEARCH ON THE ETHICAL BEHAVIOR
OF COUNSELORS

The purpose of this chapter is to provide some insights into the current state of research related to the ethical behavior of counselors. For knowledge in the area of ethics to expand and develop, research is needed to illuminate and support its theoretical base. Ideally, the theories discussed in the previous chapter should stimulate research and those subsequent research findings should contribute to the improvement of theory. As this chapter will reflect, this has not been the case for research on the ethical behavior of counselors. As Paradise (1978) has noted in commenting on this issue, there appears to be many theories with little or no research support together with research studies with no theoretical base. Hopefully, the ideas presented in this chapter may stimulate further research in this area.

Research on Counselor Ethics

The research literature on the ethical behavior of counselors is quite minimal considering the magnitude and importance of the subject matter. Ethical behavior is not a new issue for the counseling profession. Over twenty years ago Schwebel (1955) commented on the absence of research-based literature and appealed to the profession to remedy the situation. Similarly, Hobbs (1959) in a later appeal, stressed the need to critically examine the ethical behavior of the helping professions.

In an early study of the ethical decisions facing counselors, Smith (1956) asked 1,225 members of the National Vocational Guidance Association to submit critical incidents in which ethical decisions were involved. Respondents were asked questions designed to indicate the extent to which they would favor revealing confidential information to unauthorized individuals. Smith found that the greater the public school teaching experience, the greater the degree of loyalty to society and the lesser to the individual client whenever confidentiality became an issue.

Pursuing this dilemma of loyalty to the client versus loyalty to society, Wiskoff (1960) investigated what counselors would do when confronted with a conflict of loyalties. He asked three groups of psychologists, clinical, industrial and counseling, to respond to twenty-two hypothetical incidents involving conflicts of loyalty between the individual and society. His results indicated that while industrial psychologists tended to stress loyalty to society, clincial psychologists expressed their responsibility to the individual. Counseling psychologists took a position between the two.

In examining confidentiality, Nugent (1969) surveyed college counseling centers adherence to ethical codes regarding a dissemination of client information. Using a representative sample of 461 counseling centers, Nugent reported that fifty nine percent of the respondents indicated specific adherence to the ethical codes of professional organizations. However, it should be kept in mind that the possibility of socially desirable responses to Nugent's survey might more appropriately reflect what would or should be done rather than what is actually done in terms of client confidentiality.

The importance of discrimination between what counselors say they do and what they really do was demonstrated in a study by Cramer, Groff and Zani (1969). The researchers provided counselors with three hypothetical vignettes on student behavior of an educational and social nature. Counselors were then asked to write recommendations to their state universities, typical of the way in which they would ordinarily write them. The following is an example of one of the hypothetical vignettes:

> "Jane T., SAT V-630, M-670, ranks in the upper 12 percent of her graduating class. Very attractive, social, energetic, and academically talented student. Several teachers and the assistant principal reported that Jane has participated in some all night mixed couples parties. She feels that her actions are proper."

Based upon the vignettes, the responses found were quite surprising. The counselors' recommendations contained a high frequency of inappropriate material, from thirty-three to sixty seven percent of the recommendations, together with the presence of quite strong and unsupported value judgments. In addition, almost sixty percent of the counselors' recommendations contained a strong probability of academic failure despite the clear contradictory academic information contained in the hypothetical vignette. An illustrative example of this type of recommendation follows:

> ". . . . . Although Jane is an attractive and academically able student, she has some distorted values, particularly in the area of sex. There is some question in my mind concerning Jane's ability to tolerate rules and regulations at the state university . . . . ."

It should be remembered that this study described how counselors would respond to a simulated ethical dilemma, rather than to an actual one. However, the results do suggest that the rights of the client, hypothetical or not, can be easily abridged if this outcome is representative of existing practice.

The release of student information by counselors was studied by Boyd, Tennyson and Erickson (1973) and is reported with a follow-up survey conducted by the same researchers (Boyd et al., 1974). Investigating information dissemination practices, the researchers surveyed 936 of 1,074 school counselors in a midwestern state regarding the type of client information they would disseminate and to whom. The researchers found that most of the information involved was released in some form; other school personnel were likely to have unjustified access to it. They concluded from their study that counselors, in their ethical behavior, did not consider whether the information sought was theirs to give.

In their follow-up study, Boyd et al. (1974) completed another survey to assess the impact of previous information and research on the release of information. They found some evidence to conclude that there was an increase in the counselors' ethical awareness of their responsibilities in the area of confidentiality and privacy. It should be noted that when Rudolph (1968) compared school counselors to administrators and teachers on this same behavior, he found that counselors were less willing to release information about students than were teachers or administrators.

To investigate the damaging effects of nonacademic information written by counselors for college applications, Noland (1971) sent questionnaires to 200 public school counselors and to deans of admission at 405 universities. The questionnaires delineated psychological, sexual and legal infractions of school rules and regulations.

Less than twenty-five percent of the respondents stated categorically that they would *not* report emotional maladjustment on the application if it were known to them. Sixty-four percent indicated that they would. Although the results showed that counselors seemed reluctant to report incidents of sexual misbehavior, almost thirty percent indicated that they would either report it or that they were unsure as to whether it should be reported. Most counselors were definitely predisposed to reporting any legal infractions. For example, seventy percent of the counselors indicated that they would report on an application form that a young man had a juvenile record. Perhaps the most illuminating examples relevant to ethical conduct were suggested by the respondents comments in relation to reporting information. For example, "Many incidents would not be reported on the recommendation form. Such information is best submitted by personal letter or telephone." The potential impact of this type of disclosure on admission decisions is dramatic. The power of counselors in these situations can only be overshadowed by their obvious neglect of ethical considerations.

While most of the research conducted up to this point has dealt with confidentiality and the release of student information, the obvious practical question remains. If questionable practices exist, might they be due, in part, to a lack of knowledge concerning appropriate ethical behavior? Research conducted by Shertzer and Morris (1972) sheds some light on this question. To determine whether practicing counselors could discriminate between ethically appropriate and inappropriate behaviors, they prepared a questionnaire of twelve critical incidents derived from cases contained in the *Ethical Standards Casebook* (American Personnel and Guidance Association, 1965). Results obtained from sixty percent of a five percent sample of APGA members indicated that counselors could significantly discriminate appropriate from inappropriate ethical responses. It was also found that experience as a counselor was unrelated to discrimination ability. However, it should be remembered that responding to the questionnaire was voluntary so perhaps only those who were sure of their responses would, in fact, return the questionnaire. Also, the small sample size, less than three percent of the professional members, is hardly sufficient to base any firm conclusions concerning the abilities of counseling practitioners to discriminate ethical from unethical behavior.

While the present authors have been somewhat critical of the existing research, the above statements are not presented to discredit the profession, but rather to demonstrate the need for further research in an area where it is obviously justified. This research criticism should not overshadow the numerous writers who have provided important comment and insight into the issue of counselor ethics (e.g., Beck, 1971; Daubner & Daubner, 1970; Goslin, 1971; Kaplan, 1974; Ware, 1971).

New Research Directions

Most of the previous research conducted has been primarily descriptive in nature and not associated with any theoretical orientation. It would appear that if knowledge into the relevant questions of ethical behavior is to advance, theoretically-based research will be required.

A significant step in this direction was taken by Vafakas (1974) and Paradise (1976). Their research, based upon the theoretical formulations of the ethical orientation stages presented in Chapter

Three, investigated the ethical posture of practicing counselors and counselors in training. Vafakas (1974), using an early form of the Ethical Judgment Scale attempted to identify and categorize the ethical orientation of community college counselors in a large Midwestern state. Her findings indicated that the counselors reflected an institutional or societal orientation when dealing with their clients. She concluded that the values and standards of their social reference groups took precedence over the values and standards of their profession. It was also shown that the greater the years of counseling experience, the more counselors tended to function within the punishment and institutional orientation. (See Table 2, The Stages of Ethical Orientation, in Chapter Three.)

In a later study Paradise (1976), expanding the theoretical formulations underlying the Ethical Judgment Scale, sought support for the stage conceptualization of ethical orientation. He hypothesized in much the same way as Turiel's (1966) research supported Kohlberg, that the sequentiality of the ethical stages would suggest that if a counselor was moving into or away from a given ethical stage, it would be adjacent to his or her dominant or most frequently used stage of ethical reasoning. The hypothesis was supported. More importantly, he also demonstrated that counselors could be trained to make higher level ethical judgments. Using randomly assigned comparison groups, he exposed Masters-level counselors to principle (Stage V) levels of ethical reasoning by use of structured group discussions of general moral dilemmas. He compared their Ethical Judgment Scale scores to control groups who received regular classroom instruction and discussion of ethical codes. The results confirmed the efficacy of structured ethical training as a method to improve the ethical awareness of counselors.

These studies were initial attempts to provide a theoretical framework from which to view the ethical behavior of counselors. While many additional questions and issues need to be addressed, Paradise (1978), in his effort to suggest a reorientation to the study of ethics, presents several areas for further research:

(1) Is there any difference between what counselors actually do and what they perceive themselves doing?

(2) Why does unethical behavior exist?

(3) How does the ethical behavior of the counselor develop?

(4) What are the effects of counselor training programs on the ethical posture of counselors?

(5) Are counselors' ethical behaviors different in different situations?

(6) What factors in the field, if any, modify or effect counselor ethical posture?

(7) Can the ethical orientation of counselors be modified or improved by specific ethical training?

For those interested in answering these research questions, Paradise cautions against the possibility of designing research that is, itself, unethical in its approach. "Indeed, the whole question of how to do ethical research on counselor ethical behaviors is a challenging research dilemma." The essence of ethical behavior deals with how counselors *should* behave. If the profession is to be successful at implementing what *should* be, it will need a greater understanding of *what* is and *why* it is. Perhaps, research can provide those answers.

SUMMARY

The majority of research on the ethical behavior of counselors has focused on the issues of confidentiality and the release of client information. For the most part, these efforts have suggested questionable ethical practices by the profession.

The authors suggest that new research directions are needed to answer the relevant research questions concerning the ethical behavior of counselors. Several issues are provided for further research with the suggestion that a greater understanding, of *what* the ethical posture of the profession is and *why*, can be achieved through research on ethical behavior.

Chapter Five

PROBLEMS OF ETHICS in the HELPING PROFESSIONS

In the preceding chapters we have attempted to provide a theoretical background for the study of ethics in counseling and psychotherapy. Emphasis has been placed on ethical principles and upon ethical problems in a changing society. We turn now to ethical actions in the helping professions and discuss such topics as professional responsibilities of psychological counselors, ethical decision making, ethical codes, and dilemmas facing professional helpers. Following these discussions we provide several exercises and study questions which will be useful in developing an understanding of ethical problems encountered in the practice of counseling and psychotherapy. These exercises, along with the Ethical Judgment Scale (EJS) which is briefly described in the Preface, provide a solid basis for understanding the process of ethical reasoning in the helping professions. Moreover, these materials provide some concrete examples of the myriad ethical issues in the practice of counseling and psychotherapy.

The Age of Psychiatry

Some social commentators have described this century as "An Age of Psychiatry." This label may be as valid as it is descriptive.

During the past few decades the crafts of counseling and psychotherapy have achieved a position of prominence in Western society. Their professors and practitioners have advanced from positions of relative obscurity to positions of status in a period of three or four decades. Psychotherapy has gained increasing acceptance and wide appeal among all classes of people, and is generally viewed not only as a primary means for dealing with mental deviance, but also as a proper method for coping with problems of living as well (London, 1964).

It is grossly estimated that as many as 200,000 analysts, therapists, counselors and other mental health specialists earn their livelihoods ministering to the mental health needs of this nation. Other professionals, i. e., social workers, pastors, teachers, and certain health personnel, regularly provide counseling or therapy as part of their primary jobs. The costs of mental therapy in this country — in clinics, hospitals, schools, government services, and in private offices — runs into tens of millions of dollars.

There is no doubt that counselors and psychotherapists — wearing different titles and using varied approaches — have provided socially useful and personally helpful services to large numbers of people with emotional handicaps. Further, society has benefited greatly from services provided to those people with severe and malfunctional mental problems. Society has encouraged the growth of therapy and has provided financial support to most groups of therapists — psychologists, psychiatrists and counselors.

Counselors and psychotherapists wield considerable influence in numerous aspects of contemporary society. Lowe (1976) notes that counselors now perform several functions which in the past had been performed by ministers or priests. According to Lowe, the priesthood of Biblical times occupied a position between God and man, making the confrontation less fearful for men. Psychological counselors now occupy a similar position, mediating between the individual and society and conveying the meaning of that social world which is often bewildering to the modern individual. "To the therapists belong the keys of a new kingdom, whose gates are opened not by faith in the supernatural, but by faith in science as interpreter of social reality." London (1964) also suggests that the influence of the counselor is that of a secular priest whose sermon is not from revelation but from the science laboratory.

Psychotherapy is now firmly rooted in modern society and is eloquently endorsed by people of authority and influence. The work of counselors and psychotherapists has become more than just a group of services or activities performed by members of the helping professions. Therapy is a major social force and is a primary influence in our beliefs, attitudes and values. Counselors in schools and organizations, institutional psychiatrists, social workers and other psychological helpers routinely make interpretations of behvavior that influence policy making, standards of conduct, and legislation. Further, in some instances therapists exert a most direct influence upon the lives of the people they serve. As examples, psychiatrists are often asked to make recommendations on commitments to mental hospitals and counselors routinely make recommendations which determine whether people get jobs or go to college; they may often make interpretations about a person's mental ability or emotional stability. All of this adds up to authority and control over the lives of people.

There are some real dangers in this system. The first of these lies in the possibility of inaccuracies in our information about people. While the behavioral sciences have made great strides in the past century, we have only scratched the surface in our attempts to understand human behavior. Thus, much of the information used by counselors and psychotherapists is questionable, either because it is subjective or because it is capable of misinterpretation. Most of their recommendations bear the imprints of value judgments and opinions; the tendency to use psychiatric labels when describing behavior is often confusing and misleading. Although the therapists' hearts may be pure, the "facts" are often grossly inaccurate.

More precisely, therapy, unlike a science such as biology or mathematics, lacks scientific validation and solid research evidence to support the claims and activities of its practitioners. This means that much of what happens in counseling and psychotherapy depends upon "the self of the therapist" as an instrument as well as a method of treatment. Counselors have no X-ray machines and no magic pills; the therapist wields no knife and bandages no cuts. Therapists deal with illness of the mind: They treat by listening and talking. Counselors and psychotherapists deal with what clients believe and think as well as with how the clients feel.

During the past few years the state has assumed increasing responsibility for such social problems as drug abuse, alcoholism, and crime and violence, and has relied heavily upon counselors and psychotherapists as primary professionals in the treatment of these problems. Current trends suggest an expansion of counseling services in all aspects of American life.

These events and conditions serve to illustrate the influence of the helping professions on numerous aspects of modern life. There is little doubt that therapists have much to offer in the way of treating many social and human problems.

Ethics and the Law

"Ethics and the Law" defines in an indirect way the subject briefly treated in this section. More precisely we are interested in how the law influences and regulates the practice of counseling and psychotherapy and the extent to which ethical codes and standards control the professional behavior of therapists. Space does not permit a discussion of whether an immoral act, in and of itself, is sufficient reason for declaring that behavior illegal.

Ethical Codes

Ethical codes of professional associations such as the American Personnel and Guidance Association (APGA) and the American Psychological Association (APA) provide some guidelines for the professional behavior of members. These codes attempt to specify the nature of the ethical responsibilities of members. (See the Appendix.) The codes or standards formulated by professional associations represent a consensus of members' beliefs and concerns about ethical behavior. While these guidelines are quite useful to counselors and other mental health practitioners they do not always provide specific directions when ethical decisions are necessary. Ethical actions reflect the practitioners values, experiences, competency and prejudices, and while codes can provide some useful directions, only the individual can make ethical choices.

Ethical codes serve several purposes. First they protect members of the profession from practices that may result in public condemnation. Second, they provide some measure of self-regulation for the profession thus giving the professional group some freedom and autonomy. Third, they may provide clients some degree of protection from charlatans and incompetents. Finally as Fish (1973) notes, ethical codes help protect counselors or psychotherapists from the public. Adhering to the code, they have some protection if they are sued for malpractice.

Ethical standards may also help a group achieve professional status and identity. Counselors and psychotherapists sell a service rather than a product. When anyone performs a specialized service which is not easily evaluated and which is intangible, s/he incurs an obligation which is ethical in nature. In this sense the professional is distinguished not only from the amateur who is not paid, but also from the merchant who sells a product which can be weighed, measured and touched. In these circumstances therapists have a heavy obligation to provide a useful and appropriate service even though they may at times neglect to do so and go undetected in their failure.

Some professional groups have established specific procedures to be followed when their ethical code is violated. The American Psychological Association (APA), as an example, has a committee which rules on charges of unethical conduct and often expels members who are found guilty. To date, the American Personnel and Guidance Association (APGA) has no specific procedures for dealing with violations of its ethical code. Some state branches of APGA, however, are in the process of developing guidelines for dealing with unethical behavior of members.

As noted earlier ethical codes such as those mentioned here do not provide clear answers to ethical questions. They can, however, provide some useful directional guidelines and may in fact provide some legal support for some professional actions of counselors. For example, Swanson and Van Hoose (1977) cite a New York court case, *Cherry vs. Board of Regents of State of New York*, 44 N. E. 2d 405, 1974, in which the court held that in the absence of law, counselors are left to follow the suggestions of their professional associations' ethical codes.

The Influence of Legislation

In a preceding paragraph we noted the rapid growth and influence of the helping professions during the past few decades. Mental health has become a national concern and to some extent the provision of mental health services has become a responsibility of the state. This concern is manifested through public funding for community mental health centers, family and child counseling centers, outreach programs, and various counseling programs in education.

These developments have been accompanied by the passage of various laws, at both state and national levels, which have had a significant impact upon counseling and psychotherapy. To cite a few examples of federal legislation, during the past thirty years Congress has passed the Vocational Rehabilitation Act, the Community Mental Health Act, and acts establishing Medicare and Medicaid programs. In addition, legislation such as the National Defense Education Act and various federal support programs of the 1960s and 1970s provides assistance for counseling and psychological services in both elementary and secondary schools.

The myriad laws enacted during the past three or four decades have to a large extent described who can provide counseling and psychotherapy, how much therapists can be paid, and who their clients are. Forty-seven states have statutes regulating the practice of psychology through licensure or certification (Dorken, 1976). All state boards of education maintain credentialing programs for counselors, school psychologists, school social workers, and other mental health personnel working in schools. Some federal legislation names the groups of people who can receive counseling in funded programs. Among these groups are alcoholics, handicapped persons, Indians, and limited English-speaking persons. The Federal Employee Benefit Act (1974) provides for a variety of health services for federal employees including "psychological services." Providers of these services stand to receive government funds in the form of third-party payments (Ritchie, 1978).

These developments have challenged the traditional roles of counselors and have added new dimensions to the work of all helping professionals. Counselors are now deeply involved with community agencies, state supported health programs, and with the public mental health movement. This means more control and supervision by persons outside the profession. These conditions have numerous implications for the professional conduct of therapists.

Judicial Decisions

While the federal congress and the various state legislatures have passed statutes recognizing, supporting and regulating counseling and psychotherapy, the courts have also rendered numerous decisions which have direct influence upon the actions of therapists in all settings. Ritchie's (1978) review of court cases involving legal recognition of counseling revealed that during the past four years at least four courts have ruled that counseling is a legitimate service and have granted counselors the right to engage in private practice for a fee. (Here a distinction between "counselors" and other psychological helpers must be noted. While professionals such as psychologists and psychiatrists have had legal rights to practice their craft in a variety of settings for several decades, counselors not credentialed in psychology or psychiatry are just now beginning to engage in the private practice of counseling. Licensure laws granting counselors this privilege have been introduced in several states and Alabama, Arkansas and Virginia have already enacted laws licensing counselors.)

While the courts were giving legal recognition to counselors and psychotherapists they were simultaneously handing down decisions which have several implications for the professional conduct of therapists. For example in *Tarasoff vs. Regents of the University of California* (Pacific Reporter 529, P2d 553 1975), the state supreme court ruled that a university psychotherapist was "liable for failure to warn" a person threatened by his/her client. Courts have also ruled that counselors have a duty to act "skillfully" and with "due care." The client-therapist relationship has also received some attention in judicial decisions. Generally, the courts have taken a dim view of "personal" or "beyond the couch" relationships between male therapists and female clients.

The law is a part of the social process, subject to change and interpretation. It affects and is affected by social mores, beliefs and values. Courts have broad powers to interpret the law and to render decisions about the "rightness" or "wrongness" of behavior. This means, in fact, that the courts could chart the directions of the helping professions. However, it appears unlikely that they will do so.

Some ethical problems also have numerous legal implications and may often be covered by statutes or court decisions. Some examples of ethical-legal issues in the helping professions are identified as follows:

Confidentiality. The terms *private* and *confidential* have special meanings in the counseling profession. The counselor is expected to hold in confidence all matters or materials dealt with in counseling. The Code of Ethics of the American Personnel and Guidance Association contains several statements pertinent to the issue of confidentiality. For example, "The counseling relationship and information resulting therefrom shall be kept confidential, consistent with the obligations of the member as a professional person" (APGA, 1974).

The Principles of Medical Ethics, adopted by the American Psychiatric Association, deal with confidentiality as follows: "A physician may not reveal the confidences entrusted to him in the course of medical attendance, or the deficiencies he may observe in the character of the patients, unless he is required to do so by law or unless it becomes necessary to protect the welfare of the individual or of the community" (American Psychiatric Association, 1973, Sec. 6).

Statutes and court decisions as well as ethical codes have established the principle that people are entitled to keep some things private. The law clearly recognizes this right and in many cases will not permit private communication to be divulged.

There are no hard and fast legal rules governing a confidential relationship. However, as Swanson and Van Hoose (1977) have stated, there are some generalizations which can be made from court rulings related to this topic. The counselor has an ethical duty to maintain the confidence unless such information must be released to protect the client or others from harm — for example, information about dangerous drugs, suicide or planned crimes. The counselor's duty in these instances would be to reveal information in order to protect the client or others. The *Tarasoff* case, mentioned earlier in this chapter, is a good example of this requirement.

The best rule to follow in deciding when to share a confidence is the *need* for the third party to know. If the third party has a legitimate need for information in order for *necessary* action to take place, or if this third party has a corresponding legal, social, or moral interest in the client, the counselor will not be violating the client's trust or right to privacy (Swanson & Van Hoose, 1977).

Privileged Communication. Closely related to the subject of confidentiality, the application of the principle of privileged communication is sometimes an issue in counseling. Legally, privileged communication can be defined as communications which are confidential because of a special relationship.

In the history of privileged communication the legal tradition allowed for only two relationships in which the privilege against speaking out in court could be applied: husband-wife, and attorney-client. Over the years this rule has been extended to physician-patient, counselor-client, and psychologist-client.

In the absence of statutes counselors can be required to appear in court to testify about communications with clients. Further, there are numerous exceptions in the privileged communication rule. For example, even with a protective statute, it is generally held that the element of confidentiality must be essential to the relationship and that damage to the relationship would occur by disclosure. Courts have broad power to interpret the law and in this instance to determine whether the rule applies.

As noted earlier, ethical standards of the helping professions quite clearly prohibit disclosure except in cases of threat of harm to clients or others. Rigid adherence to these principles may place the counselor in a position that would lead to a charge of contempt of court. This is of course a moral dilemma, but it is by no means among the greatest dilemmas that professional counselors face.

Malpractice. Malpractice is most often discussed in a legal context and thus may seem out of place in a text on ethics. We have focused upon the actions of counselors and psychotherapists and upon principles of ethical conduct. Malpractice relates directly to the actions of helping professionals and in our view is intricately linked to moral and ethical actions of therapists. Further, there are some indications that counselors may become increasingly susceptible to lawsuits for malpractice; thus, it is helpful to provide some perspective on this emerging problem. As with other topics, our treatment of malpractice is not intended to be exhaustive. We refer the interested reader to several books and articles dealing with this issue, some of which are found in the bibliography.

Malpractice, as used here, is defined as improper or negligent treatment or service which results in bodily, mental, or monetary injury to another person. The concept is based upon several ancient and medieval laws which held that an injured party was entitled to some form of retribution from the offender. In some instances if a practitioner's actions caused injury to a client s/he also must suffer physical injury. Some ancient legal codes dealt specifically with medical malpractice. "A surgeon who caused the loss of a limb may lose his hand. Surgeons carried no liability insurance but one guesses they were pretty careful" (Barchilon, 1975). In modern times, both statute and case law permits the injured party to take legal action in an effort to compensate for the alleged injury.

Three conditions must be present in malpractice litigation. First, the defendant must have a *duty* to the plaintiff; second, *damages* must result through *negligence* or improper performance of that duty, and finally there must be a *causal relationship* between damages and negligence (Dawidoff, 1973).

The major attributes of malpractice are failure to act properly, failure to use due care, and negligence. The key word in malpractice is *negligence* and according to Dawidoff, aside from some minor differences, malpractice resembles conventional negligence in every respect.

Malpractice actions against counselors and psychotherapists are infrequent when compared to lawsuits against other groups such as physicians. However, the incidence of malpractice suits against therapists appears to be increasing. We know that counselors in schools and colleges have been hauled into court on negligence charges based on failure to warn, and failure to use care. Psychologists and psychiatrists in private practice and in institutional settings report that the prevalence of damage suits has risen sharply in recent years.

The best safeguard against malpractice is professional and personal honesty. Some understanding of one's limitations as well as a sense of duty to society should contravene some of the potential problems in therapist liability.

Ethical Decision-making

As we alluded to in earlier chapters, every counselor operates from his or her own personal style of ethics. Generally, this is sufficient for the most part. It is only when one is faced with a dilemma for which there is no apparent good or best solution that problems arise. It is for this reason that counselors need to understand and develop their own process for ethical decision-making.

The universal or absolute models of ethical conduct suggested by the theorists, the law, society, or the professional organizations may not always be totally compatible with the counselor's own system of morality. Browne (1973) aptly justifies the necessity for a well-defined ethical decision making process for the individual:

> "When you decide to take matters into your own hands, someone may ask you: . . . . . Who are you to decide for yourself in the face of society and centuries of moral teachings?"
> "The answer is simple: You are you, the person who will live with the consequences of what you do. . . . . . You have to be the one to decide. . . . . . You have to know."

Browne, in commenting on the "morality trap," the irrational belief that people *must* obey an ethical code created by someone else, encourages the individual to reassess the relevant consequences of personal action and construct his or her own personal morality to guide behavior. As Van Hoose and Kottler (1977) ominously note, it is the blind obedience to authority which is responsible for some of history's greatest tragedies.

For the counselor, nearly every intervention, indeed, almost everything said and done, has potential ethical ramifications. Therefore, an appropriate rationale for all counselor actions is always important. To help counselors understand the basic reasoning underlying their actions was one of the central purposes for the development of the Ethical Judgment Scale. As discussed in an earlier chapter, the reasoning underlying counselor judgments related to ethical dilemmas may be attributed to five qualitatively different ethical orientations:

(a) *Stage I:* Absolute dogmatic beliefs of right and wrong, good and bad.

(b) *Stage II:* Right and wrong as defined by higher authorities.

(c) *Stage III:* Right and wrong as defined by societal or legal expectations.

(d) *Stage IV:* Right and wrong as defined by what is best for the client, considering the societal and legal ramifications.

(e) *Stage V:* Right and wrong as defined by general principles of conscience regardless of legal and societal consequences.

This framework is presented as a model from which the individual should explore his or her own rationale for the particular moral and ethical judgments that have been made or need to be made. Utilizing this approach can serve as the first step in synthesizing a personal system of moral and ethical behavior. Later in this chapter, several exercises are presented to help the reader explore the underlying rationale for the moral and ethical judgments that he or she may make. Hopefully, insight and self-awareness into the underlying reasoning of one's actions will stimulate greater levels of ethical judgments.

Models for Ethical Decision Making

Proposed models or approaches to ethical decision making span centuries – from Bentham's initial problem solving approach discussed in Chapter Three to the systems analysis flow chart developed by Van Hoose and Kottler (1977). They all appear to be basic modifications to Bentham's utilitarian analysis of consequences procedure.

More importantly, they all suffer from the same limitation of which John Stuart Mill noted that sufficient time to adequately reflect and consider all consequences may not be available. This is particularly true for the work of the counselor, where sometimes only seconds or minutes exist between interventions having possible ethical implications for the client. It is for this very reason that the therapist needs to devote time to analyzing his or her professional behavior. Only in this way will greater ethical responsibility develop.

Whatever approach to analyzing one's ethical decision making is used, it should involve the following elements:

(a) *Identify the problem or dilemma.* What is the source of conflict? Is it between the client and society, the client and the institution, the institution and society, etc.? The ethical orientations presented earlier can help in accurately identifying where the conflict lies. What is contributing to the source of doubts about possible courses of action?

Often counselors do not realize they are facing an ethical dilemma until it is too late. Obviously, the best way to overcome this problem is to be thoroughly familiar with the responsibilities of the profession and its ethical codifications.

(b) *Do any rules or guiding principles exist to help resolve the dilemma?* When there are expectations or rules, whether for the institution, society, or the standards of the profession, the individual's agreement with these guidelines must be examined. Perhaps guidelines exist that are in conflict with the counselor's own personal expectations.

It is also true that for many ethical dilemmas, no specific rules or guidelines will apply. Examining the ethical codes of the profession (see the Appendices) will suggest many problems which are not addressed. When this is the case, as frequently happens, it is always wise to consult other professional colleagues and supervisory personnel for their opinions and, if necessary, get competent legal advice. The legal dimensions of counseling have not been that clearly defined. Whenever ethical judgments have potential legal implications, whether civil or criminal, competent legal advice is always important to the decision making process.

(c) *Generate possible and probable courses of action.* List the courses of action that are possible and probable so that each may be examined from the perspective of its underlying rationale. Here the rationale for the stages of ethical orientation may be of help.

(d) *Consider potential consequences for each course of action.* What are the implications and ramifications of each course of action? How likely is each consequence to occur? Another important issue to consider in this element of the process is where and to whom your responsibilities lie — to the individual, to society, to the institution, to your supervisor, etc.? Are you serving your needs or someone else's?

(e) *Select the best course of action.* Once decided, it is your decision to live with. As Browne (1973) warns, "If you are wrong, you will suffer for it. If you're right, you will find happiness." This is precisely why one must be ready to justify actions in an appropriate and meaningful way.

Since there is no universally accepted explication of right and wrong conduct, some personal ethical system is always necessary for the professional. This model can prove valuable to therapists who wish to work out their own system of ethical beliefs and practices. One rule of thumb for use of this model is presented for consideration: The counselor or psychotherapist is *probably* acting in an ethically responsible way concerning a client if (1) he or she has maintained personal and professional honesty, coupled with (2) the best interests of the client, (3) without malice or personal gain, and (4) can justify his or her actions as the best judgment of what should be done based upon the current state of the profession. Whenever these four components are present, ethically responsible behavior is likely to be demonstrated.

Some additional questions that may be useful in the development of a personal ethical system have been adapted from Van Hoose and Kottler (1977). They include the following items for ethical self-evaluation:

1. Was the guideline, code or expectation devised to restrain you or was it developed to aid in your professional development?

2. Have you accepted the guidelines because they have always been present or because you have personally determined that they are in consonance with your own value system?

3. What would you be willing to do for money — for example, continuing a client relationship when you are aware that you can no longer be of any meaningful help?

4. Upon what values are the rewards and payoffs, which you obtain from your work as a counselor, based?

5. Under what circumstances would you lie to a client?

6. To what extent would you attempt to provide services for which you are not properly trained or experienced?

7. When would you find it necessary to divulge confidential information?

8. How tolerant are you of the unethical practices of your colleagues? Under what circumstances would you take action?

9. How often do you use the counselor-client relationship to satisfy your own needs?

10. By what method do you evaluate your effectiveness?

11. How would you handle situations of transference and counter-transference with clients of the opposite sex?

12. To what extent do your own personal problems interfere with your work as a counselor?

13. Are you more interested in young, attractive, verbal clients than those who are not so young, not so attractive, and not so verbal?

Some of these questions should require you to pause and take stock of yourself. That is their purpose. They have no simple, easy answers. To further help you in this effort we have presented at the end of this chapter two exercises on ethical decision making. They should encourage further reflection and self-examination as well as provide additional familiarity with the ethical standards of the profession.

SUMMARY

It is our belief that a systematic and meaningful approach to ethical judgments, justifiable on the basis of universally-accepted principles of human conscience, will:

- Prevent actions that vary as the situations vary.

- Not change as the authority figures in the situations change.

- Not be based upon unquestioned adherence to someone else's proscriptions and expectations.

Exercise One

Read the following case summaries of ethical dilemmas and respond to the questions posed at the end of each summary. After you
have answered each question read the American Personnel and Guidance Association (APGA) and American Psychological Association
(APA) codes of ethics contained in the Appendix. You may wish
to review your answers to the questions posed in the dilemmas.

The Ethical Dilemma of Counselor A

Background

Counselor A is working in a community college. For the past
two months he has been seeing James C., a student, in individual
vocational counseling sessions. During the course of the interviews
James has confessed that for several years he has been cheating on
tests in order to receive good grades; he can then transfer to a presti-
gious university where he can complete his bachelor's degree.

James has complained that increasing parental pressure to receive good grades has made him a "basket case." He has related incidents in which he has become so nervous at the prospect of taking
an exam that the only way he can "calm down" is by devising ways
to cheat.

James has tried to talk to his parents about their continual
"pushing" for achievement, but his efforts have met with failure.
He is afraid that if he cannot transfer to a well-known school, his
parents, both with advanced degrees, will never forgive him. He also
fears that unless he has perfect grades he will never realize his career
goal of becoming a journalist.

James is a likeable person and very popular at the college. His
friends and teachers have great respect for his abilities and personal
qualities. James has been so anxious about living up to everyone's
expectations that he has started using alcohol quite excessively.

During his first interview with Counselor A, James was very
concerned that what he said would not be held in confidence. Counselor A, sensing that James was experiencing considerable difficulties,
reassured him of the confidentiality of the interview. Later, a high
degree of professional rapport is evidenced.

The Problem

James is caught cheating on an exam by his history professor.
After the class, James pleads with the professor for consideration,
claiming that he has never cheated before and will never do so again.

The professor, believing that James is sincere, is undecided about what to do. He seeks the opinion of the dean of the school as to possible courses of action.

The dean, who is a personal friend of James' parents, is unsure about what to recommend and asks for some time to consider the situation. Noting that James' college counselor is Counselor A, he writes a memo to the counselor, explaining the cheating matter. He asks that Counselor A reach a decision about the situation quickly. In the memo, he also asks Counselor A the following questions:

(a)   Are you familiar with James?

(b)   Have you seen James for counseling?

(c)   Did you have any knowledge of possible reasons for this behavior?

(d)   Are you aware of any previous cheating or serious rule violation?

(e)   Would you recommend that James be allowed to retake the exam, fail the exam, or fail the course?

(f)   Would you be willing to see James as a professional counselor acting for the dean's office.

The Dilemma

Counselor A has been placed in a precarious position by James' action and the dean's request. Should he inform the dean of his knowledge of James? Should he use the issue of confidentiality to deny the request? A denial might even confirm any suspicions that the dean might have. If he denies any knowledge of James, how can he see him, acting as the dean's representative? Counselor A fears that his job could be at stake along with his professional identity.

To help decide what Counselor A should do, answer the following questions:

1.   What are the counselor's responsibilities to James? ....

....

....

....

....

....

....

2.   What are the counselor's responsibilities to the dean? ....

....

....

....

....

....

3.   What are the counselor's responsibilities to the institution?

....

....

....

....

....

4.   What are his responsibilities to society, that is, James' fellow students in the history class who did not cheat? ....

....

....

....

....

5.   What are the counselor's responsibilities to James' parents?

....

....

....

....

....

6. What are the counselor's responsibilities to his profession?

....

....

....

....

7. Review the APGA and APA ethical codes set forth in the
    Appendix.   Look for any statements that may apply to this
    case. How would these affect your decision? Be specific.

....

....

....

....

....

....

8. Generate possible alternative courses of action stating why they
    are chosen.   ....

....

....

....

....

....

....

9. What are the possible and probable consequences of each course
   of action? ....

....

....

....

....

....

....

....

....

10. For the courses of action you have listed in answer to the eighth
    question, name the stage of ethical development each suggests.
    Explain. ....

....

....

....

....

....

....

....

....

....

The Ethical Dilemma of Counselor B

Background

Counselor B is working as a youth services counselor for the Child Welfare Board of an urban city. She has been asked by the court to see ten-year-old Nancy L. to determine if she should be returned to the custody of her mother. Nancy L. has been living with foster parents for the past two years.

The foster parents, Mr. and Mrs. S., have become quite attached to Nancy and have initiated legal proceedings to adopt her. Shortly after they informed the Child Welfare Board of their intentions, Nancy's natural mother, Mrs. L., hired a lawyer to regain custody of her daughter.

Nancy had been sent to live with her foster parents after her mother was convicted of prostitution. After serving six months, Mrs. L. was paroled and began working in a department store. She has recently married a former boyfriend. They have been married for almost a year and would like to have Nancy live with them.

For several weeks, Counselor B has been seeing all parties in-involved in the situation. The following background information has been obtained: Nancy has a loving relationship with her foster parents and does not want to be separated from them, even though she believes them to be very strict parents. During the first year that Nancy lived with them, her mother made no attempts to contact her or to see her. The foster parents believe that it was only after the mother learned of the impending adoption that she began to take an interest in her daughter. Counselor B has also learned through a former neighbor of Nancy's mother that the man Mrs. L. has married was also involved in the prostitution activities that caused her arrest. However, in talking with Mrs. L. and her new husband, it was determined that both seem sincere in their desire to have Nancy in their home. Mrs. L. and her husband feel that Mrs. L. has paid for her past actions and that she has a right to have custody of her daughter. Mrs. L. states that prison was a very difficult adjustment for her and that it took some time for her to "get back on her feet." This is why she did not attempt to contact her daughter earlier. Mrs. L.'s husband claims he has a good job that will support Nancy and her mother and that Mrs. L. will be able to stay at home and devote her attentions to Nancy. Although he had some minor scrapes with the law as a juvenile, and although the police suspect him of continued involvement in prostitution, he has no police record.

The court would like the counselor's recommendation, as to whether Nancy should be returned to the custody of her natural mother, as soon as possible.

The Problem

Should the counselor recommend that Nancy be returned to her mother overriding Nancy's wishes to remain with her foster parents? While Nancy's natural mother appears to be making a constructive change in her life, there is some suspicion as to whether this is really the case. Counselor B has also learned from the Child Welfare Agency that several unsubstantiated complaints have been filed against Mr. and Mrs. D., the foster parents, for the apparent harsh discipline they have exercised on previous children in their care.

The Dilemma

Should a mother be deprived of her child? Should Counselor B act on her suspicions about Nancy's mother and step-father? Does Mrs. L. deserve to be punished again for past actions? What would you recommend? Why? To help you decide what Counselor B should do, answer the following questions:

1.   Exactly who is Counselor B's Client? ....

....

....

2.   What are the counselor's responsibilities to Nancy? ....

....

....

....

3.   What are the counselor's responsibilities to Nancy's natural mother? ....

....

....

....

....

....

4. What impact do the wishes of ten-year-old Nancy have upon Counselor B's recommendation? ....

....

....

....

....

5. What are the counselor's responsibilities to the court? ....

....

....

....

....

....

6. What are the counselor's responsibilities to society, i. e., the welfare of this child and others like her? ....

....

....

....

....

7. Generate possible alternative courses of action stating why they were chosen. ....

....

....

....

....

....

8. What are the *possible* and *probable* consequences of the actions that Counselor B could take? ....

....

....

....

....

9. Review the APGA and APA ethical codes in the Appendix and look for any statements that may apply to this case. How would these affect your decision? Be specific. . . . .

....

....

....

....

10. For the courses of action you have listed in answer to the eighth question, name the stage of ethical development each suggests. Explain. ....

....

....

....

11. As Counselor B, what would you do and why? ....

....

....

....

....

The Ethical Dilemma of Counselor C

Background

Counselor C is a community mental health counselor at a locally funded family counseling agency in an urban city. He belongs to a labor union for municipal employees. He has a large caseload of clients as do all the counselors at the agency.

When the union to which he belongs votes to strike for better working conditions and higher pay he supports the action because he feels that the excessive caseloads and poor working conditions ultimately do a disservice to the clients who come to the agency. However, he begins to have second thoughts about the impact of the strike action upon his clients, many of whom have been coming to the agency regularly with relatively severe emotional concerns.

He discusses his feelings with co-workers after the union decides to strike against the local agency and they are unsympathetic. They tell him that as a member of the union, he has agreed to abide by the vote and that unless a unified action can be taken, the city will never agree to improve the situation. They also tell him, in no uncertain terms, that he should not disregard the picket line that will be at the agency; doing so could cause some problems in the future. He suspects that since his supervisor is also the spokesman for this group in the union, he could have some difficulties. He also firmly believes that the demands of the union are justified and ultimately, in the best interests of the clients served by the agency.

The Problem

Should Counselor C go on strike as he has previously agreed or should he disobey the strike order and continue to see his clients at the agency?

The Dilemma

Counselor C has an ethical dilemma in terms of his decision to continue serving his clients under conditions he feels should be improved or to engage in a strike activity which is supported by all of the agency's counselors. His decision is further complicated by the fact that he believes the demands of the union are justified in order to provide adequate services for the clients.

To help decide what Counselor C should do, answer the following questions:

1. Are there any specific ethical standards that could apply to this situation? (Review APGA and APA ethical standards contained in the Appendix.) ....

....

....

....

....

....

2. Are any of these standards in conflict with one another in this particular situation? Explain. . . . .

....

....

....

....

....

3. What are the counselor's responsibilities to his clients? . . . .

....

....

....

....

....

....

4. What are the counselor's responsibilities to his union, his colleagues, and the possible further improvement of counseling services as a result of the strike? ....

....

....

....

....

....

5. Will his actions have any impact upon the situation in terms of the strike occurring and the overall handling of clients during the strike? ....

....

....

....

....

6. What are the counselor's responsibilities to society, that is, the local population which the agency serves? ....

....

....

....

....

....

....

....

7. What are the counselor's responsibilities to the counseling pro-
    fession? ....

    ....

    ....

    ....

    ....

8. Generate possible alternative courses of action, stating why they
    were chosen. ....

    ....

    ....

    ....

    ....

9. What are the *possible* and *probable* consequences of each course
    of action that Counselor C could take? ....

    ....

    ....

    ....

    ....

    ....

    ....

    ....

10. For the courses of action you have listed in answer to the eighth question, name the stage of ethical development each suggests. Explain. ....

....

....

....

....

....

....

....

....

....

11. As Counselor C, what would you do and why? ....

....

....

....

....

....

....

....

....

....

Exercise Two

The following case vignettes are based upon the American Personnel and Guidance Association (APGA) Ethical Standards. (See Appendix A.)   After you have read each vignette, read the section of the ethical code to which it applies and answer the discussion questions. Discuss your answers in small groups. You may also wish to compare the ethical positions stated by the APGA with those of the APA (American Psychological Association). [See Appendix B.]

Case A

A counselor makes unreasonable and unsubstantiated claims about the effectiveness of his recently developed counseling techniques, stating that research on their effectiveness suggests startling advances for marital counseling. The counselor is unable to produce any research documents to support his claims.

See Section A.1, A.4.

1.   Is this behavior unethical? If so, why? ....

....

....

....

....

2.   What would be the consequences of this behavior? ....

....

....

....

....

3.   What suggestions could you make to rectify the situation?

....

....

....

....

....

4.   What action would you take if you became aware of this situation? ....

....

....

....

....

Case B

A counselor becomes aware that a co-worker is offering marriage counseling, privately, for a fee to clients who could otherwise obtain help from the agency for whom they both work. The counselor feels that his co-worker is using his position to recruit possible clients for his private practice.

See Section A.3, A.6, E.7.

1.   Is this behavior unethical? If so, why? . . . .

....

....

....

....

....

2.   What could be the consequences of this behavior? ....

....

....

....

....

....

3.   What suggestions could you make to rectify the situation?

....

....

....

....

4.   What action would you take if you became aware of this
     situation?   ....

....

....

....

....

Case C

A counselor with a Master's degree in music education is using a
business card that states, "M. A. Vocational Counseling." He claims
that although he has his Master's degree in music, he has taken several graduate courses in counseling and has, in fact, the equivalent
number of vocational counseling courses for certification. Since
there is no counselor licensing law in his state, he feels free to offer
vocational counseling to the public.

See Section A.5.

1. Is this behavior unethical? If so, why? ....

....

....

....

....

2. What could be the consequences of this behavior? ....

....

....

....

....

3. What suggestions could you make to rectify this situation?

....

....

....

....

4. What action would you take if you became aware of this situation? ....

....

....

....

....

....

Case D

A university counselor has been confronted with certain unethical research practices involving the use of students in research
studies without sufficient safeguards for their anonymity or possible
emotional well-being. He claims that he is not a member of APGA
and therefore is not bound by their ethical code.

See Section A.3, D.4, D.5.

1.   Is this behavior unethical? If so, why? ....

....

....

....

....

2.   Can action be taken against an individual for violating an ethical
     code of an organization, if the individual is not a member? . . . .

....

....

....

....

3.   Suggest types of action that could be taken. ....

....

....

....

....

4. What action would you take if you became aware of this situation? ....

....

....

....

....

Case E

A counselor recommends that a client go into group counseling. As the newest member of the group, the client suffers considerable emotional trauma because of her inability to deal with feedback. She complains that the group is always attacking her and that the counselor allows this to happen. The counselor claims that the client has numerous problems with social relationships and that this is the best possible treatment for her. The client subsequently terminates the group and begins seeing another counselor in individual counseling.

See Section B.1.

1. Is this behavior unethical? If so, why? ....

....

....

....

....

2. What could be the consequences of this behavior? ....

....

....

....

....

....

3. What suggestions could you make to rectify this situation?

....

....

....

....

4. What action would you take if you became aware of this situation? ....

....

....

....

....

Case F

During vocational counseling with a client, a counselor learns that the client is under the care of a psychiatrist. The counselor does not contact the psychiatrist for consent because she feels that she is doing vocational counseling, not psychotherapy and it is up to the client to decide who he wants to see and which problems he wishes to resolve.

See Section B.3.

1. Is this behavior unethical? If so, why? ....

....

....

....

....

2.   What could be the consequences of this behavior?   . ...

....

....

....

....

3.   What suggestions could you make to rectify the situation?

....

....

....

....

4.   What action would you take if you became aware of this situation? ....

....

....

....

....

....

Case G

During a marriage counseling session an aggressive male client confesses to the counselor that if his wife goes through with her planned divorce action he may possibly become so upset that he could kill her. He admits that on several occasions he has physically abused his wife, but that he is always able to restrain himself from injuring her seriously. Since the counselor does not know the wife and is unsure as to the validity of his client's statements, he does nothing.

See Section B.4, B.11.

1.   Is this behavior unethical? If so, why? ....

....

....

....

....

2.   What could be the consequences of this behavior? ....

....

....

....

....

3.   What suggestions could you make to rectify this situation?

....

....

....

....

....

4.   What action would you take if you became aware of this
      situation? ....

....

....

....

....

....

Case H

A counselor uses an audio tape of a client with sexual problems as a demonstration of counseling techniques for a class he is teaching at a university. During the course of the tape, certain personal information is conveyed which could identify the client to the class.

See Section B.5, B.6.

1. Is this behavior unethical? If so, why? ....
....

....

....

....

2. What could be the consequences of this behavior?...............................
....

....

....

....

3. What suggestions could you make to rectify this situation?
....

....

....

....

4.   What action would you take if you became aware of this
     situation? ....

....

....

....

....

Case I

A former client of a counselor writes to request that the results
of an IQ test she has taken be sent to her. Since the counselor cannot locate the test results, he sends the client, who now happens to
be a school counselor herself, a group intelligence test with the scoring key and the manual, requesting their return with any questions
that the former client may have.

See Section A.4, A.5, A.8.

1.   Is this behavior unethical? If so, why? ....

....

....

....

....

2.   What could be the consequences of this behavior? ....

....

....

....

....

....

3.   What suggestions could you make to rectify the situation?

....

....

....

....

4.   What action would you take if you became aware of this situation? ....

....

....

....

....

Case J

A professor of counseling requires that the counselor trainees, enrolled in his group counseling course, participate in two marathon encounter group sessions under his direction as part of their requirements for the course. The professor justifies this action as a method that allows him to determine if any of the trainees have personal problems that could interfere with their practice as counselors.

See Section G.4, G.5, G.12.

1.   Is this behavior unethical? If so, why? ....

....

....

....

....

....

2.   What could be the consequences of this behavior? ....

....

....

....

....

....

....

3.   What suggestions could you make to rectify the situation?

....

....

....

....

....

4.   What action would you take if you became aware of this
     situation? ....

....

....

....

....

....

....

APPENDIX A

AMERICAN PERSONNEL AND GUIDANCE ASSOCIATION

Ethical Standards

PREAMBLE

The American Personnel and Guidance Association is an educational, scientific, and professional organization whose members are dedicated to the enhancement of the worth, dignity, potential, and uniqueness of each individual and thus to the service of society.

The Association recognizes that the role definitions and work settings of its members include a wide variety of academic disciplines, levels of academic disciplines, levels of academic preparation, and agency services. This diversity reflects the breadth of the Association's interest and influence. It also poses challenging complexities in efforts to set standards for the performance of members, desired requisite preparation or practice, and supporting social, legal, and ethical controls.

The specification of ethical standards enables the Association to clarify to present and future members and to those served by members the nature of ethical responsibilities held in common by its members.

The existence of such standards serves to stimulate greater concern by members for their own professional functioning and for the conduct of fellow professionals such as counselors, guidance and student personnel workers, and others in the helping professions. As the ethical code of the Association this document establishes principles which define the ethical behavior of Association members.

Section A: **General**

1.   The member influences the development of the profession by continuous efforts to improve professional practices, teaching, services, and research. Professional growth is continuous throughout the member's career and is exemplified by the development of a philosophy that explains why and how a member functions in the helping relationship. Members are expected to gather data on their effectiveness and to be guided by the findings.

2.   The member has a responsibility both to the individual who is served and to the institution within which the service is performed. The acceptance of employment in an institution implies that the member is in substantial agreement with the general policies and principles of the institution. Therefore the professional activities of the member are also in accord with the objectives of the institution. If, despite concerted efforts, the member cannot reach agreement with the employer as to acceptable standards of conduct that allow for changes in institutional policy conducive to the positive growth and development of counselees, then terminating the affiliation should be seriously considered.

Reprinted by permission of the American Personnel and Guidance Association.

3.   Ethical behavior among professional associates, members and non-members, is expected at all times. When information is possessed which raises serious doubt as to the ethical behavior of professional colleagues, whether Association members or not, the member is obligated to take action to attempt to rectify such a condition. Such action shall utilize the institution's channels first and then utilize procedures established by the state, division, or Association.

The member can take action in a variety of ways: conferring with the in-dividual in question, gathering further information as to the allegation, confer-ring with local or national ethics committees, and so forth.

4.   The member must not seek self-enhancement through expressing evaluations or comparisons that are damaging to others.

5.   The member neither claims nor implies professional qualifications exceeding those possessed and is responsible for correcting any misrepresenta-tions of these qualifications by others.

6.   In establishing fees for professional services, members should take in-to consideration the fees charged by other professions delivering comparable services, as well as the ability of the counselee to pay. Members are willing to provide some services for which they receive little or no financial remuneration, or remuneration in food, lodging, and materials. When fees include charges for items other than professional services, that portion of the total which is for the professional services should be clearly indicated.

7.   When members provide information to the public or to subordinates, peers, or supervisors, they have a clear responsibility to ensure that the content is accurate, unbiased, and consists of objective factual data.

8.   The member shall make a careful distinction between the offering of counseling services as opposed to public information services. Counseling may be offered only in the context of a reciprocal or face-to-face relationship. In-formation services may be offered through the media.

9.   With regard to professional employment, members are expected to accept only positions that they are prepared to assume and then to comply with established practices of the particular type of employment setting in which they are employed in order to ensure the continuity of services.

Section B: Counselor-Counselee Relationship

This section refers to practices involving individual and/or group coun-seling relationships, and it is not intended to be applicable to practices in-volving administrative relationships.

To the extent that the counselee's choice of action is not imminently self- or other- destructive, the counselee must retain freedom of choice. When the counselee does not have full autonomy for reasons of age, mental incompetency, criminal incarceration, or similar legal restrictions, the member may have to work with others who exercise significant control and direction over the coun-selee. Under these circumstances the member must apprise counselees of re-strictions that may limit their freedom of choice.

1.   The member's primary obligation is to respect the integrity and promote the welfare of the counselee(s), whether the counselee(s) is (are) assisted individually or in a group relationship. In a group setting, the member-leader is also responsible for protecting individuals from physical and/or psychological trauma resulting from interaction within the group.

2.   The counseling relationship and information resulting therefrom must be kept confidential, consistent with the obligations of the member as a professional person. In a group counseling setting the member is expected to set a norm of confidentiality regarding all group participants' disclosures.

3.   If an individual is already in a counseling/therapy relationship with another professional person, the member does not begin a counseling relationship without first contacting and receiving the approval of that other professional. If the member discovers that the counselee is in another counseling/ therapy relationship after the counseling relationship begins, the member is obligated to gain the consent of the other professional or terminate the relationship, unless the counselee elects to terminate the other relationship.

4.   When the counselee's condition indicates that there is clear and imminent danger to the counselee or others, the member is expected to take direct personal action or to inform responsible authorities. Consultation with other professionals should be utilized where possible. Direct interventions, especially the assumption of responsibility for the counselee, should be taken only after careful deliberation. The counselee should be involved in the resumption of responsibility for his actions as quickly as possible.

5.   Records of the counseling relationship including interview notes, test data, correspondence, tape recordings, and other documents are to be considered professional information for use in counseling, and they are not part of the public or official records of the institution or agency in which the counselor is employed. Revelation to others of counseling material should occur only upon the express consent of the counselee.

6.   Use of data derived from a counseling relationship for purposes of counselor training or research shall be confined to content that can be sufficiently disguised to ensure full protection of the identity of the counselee involved.

7.   Counselees shall be informed of the conditions under which they may receive counseling assistance at or before the time when the counseling relationship is entered. This is particularly so when conditions exist of which the counselee would be unaware. In individual and group situations particularly those oriented to self-understanding or growth, the member-leader is obligated to make clear the purposes, goals, techniques, rules of procedure, and limitations of the relationship.

8.   The member has the responsibility to screen prospective group participants, especially when the emphasis is on self-understanding and growth through self-disclosure. The member should maintain an awareness of the group participants' compatibility throughout the life of the group.

9. The member reserves the right to consult with any other profession-ally competent person about a counselee. In choosing a consultant, the member avoids choosing a consultant in a conflict of interest situation that would pre-clude the consultant's being a proper party to the member's efforts to help the counselee.

10. If the member is unable to be of professional assistance to the counselee, the member avoids initiating the counseling relationship or the member terminates it. In either event, the member is obligated to refer the counselee to an appropriate specialist. (It is incumbent upon the member to be knowledgeable about referral resources so that a satisfactory referral can be initiated.) In the event the counselee declines the suggested referral, the mem-ber is not obligated to continue the relationship.

11. When the member learns from counseling relationships of conditions that are likely to harm others, the member should report the condition to the responsible authority. This should be done in such a manner as to conceal the identity of the counselee.

12. When the member has other relationships, particularly of an ad-ministrative, supervisory, and/or evaluative nature, with an individual seeking counseling services, the member should not serve as the counselor but should refer the individual to another professional. Only in instances where such an alternative is unavailable and where the individual's condition definitely war-rants counseling intervention should the member enter into and/or maintain a counseling relationship.

13. All experimental methods of treatment must be clearly indicated to prospective recipients, and safety precautions are to be adhered to by the member.

14. When the member is engaged in short-term group treatment/training programs, e.g., marathons and other encounter-type or growth groups, the member ensures that there is professional assistance available during and follow-ing the group experience.

15. Should the member be engaged in a work setting that calls for any variation from the above statements, the member is obligated to consult with other professionals whenever possible to consider justifiable alternatives. The variations that may be necessary should be clearly communicated to other pro-fessionals and prospective counselees.

Section C: **Measurement and Evaluation**

The primary purpose of educational and psychological testing is to provide descriptive measures that are objective and interpretable in either comparative or absolute terms. The member must recognize the need to interpret the state-ments that follow as applying to the whole range of appraisal techniques in-cluding test and nontest data. Test results constitute only one of a variety of pertinent sources of information for personnel, guidance, and counseling decisions.

1. It is the member's responsibility to provide adequate orientation or information to the examinee(s) prior to and following the test administration so that the results of testing may be placed in proper perspective with other relevant factors. In so doing, the member must recognize the effects of socioeconomic, ethnic, and cultural factors on test scores. It is the member's professional responsibility to use additional unvalidated information cautiously in modifying interpretation of the test results.

2. In selecting tests for use in a given situation or with a particular counselee, the member must consider carefully the specific validity, reliability, and appropriateness of the test(s). "General" validity, reliability, and the like may be questioned legally as well as ethically when tests are used for vocational and educational selection, placement, or counseling.

3. When making any statements to the public about tests and testing, the member is expected to give accurate information and to avoid false claims or misconceptions. Special efforts are often required to avoid unwarranted connotations of such terms as IQ and grade equivalent scores.

4. Different tests demand different levels of competence for administration, scoring, and interpretation. Members have a responsibility to recognize the limits of their competence and to perform only those functions for which they are prepared.

5. Tests should be administered under the same conditions that were established in their standardization. When tests are not administered under standard conditions or when unusual behavior or irregularities occur during the testing session, those conditions should be noted and the results designated as invalid or of questionable validity. Unsupervised or inadequately supervised test-taking, such as the use of tests through the mails, is considered unethical. On the other hand, the use of instruments that are so designed or standardized to be self-administered and self-scored, such as interest inventories, is to be encouraged.

6. The meaningfulness of test results used in personnel, guidance, and counseling functions generally depends on the examinee's unfamiliarity with the specific items on the test. Any prior coaching or dissemination of the test materials can invalidate test results. Therefore, test security is one of the professional obligations of the member. Conditions that produce the most favorable results should be made known to the examinee.

7. The purpose of testing and the explicit use of the results should be made known to the examinee prior to testing. The counselor has a responsibility to ensure that instrument limitations are not exceeded and that periodic review and/or retesting are made to prevent counselee stereotyping.

8. The examinee's welfare and explicit prior understanding should be the criteria for determining the recipients of the test results. The member is obligated to see that adequate interpretation accompanies any release of individual or group test data. The interpretation of test data should be related to the examinee's particular concerns.

9. The member is expected to be cautious when interpreting the results of research instruments possessing insufficient technical data. The specific purposes for the use of such instruments must be stated explicitly to examinees.

10. The member must proceed with extreme caution when attempting to evaluate and interpret the performance of minority group members or other persons who are not represented in the norm group on which the instrument was standardized.

11. The member is obligated to guard against the appropriation, reproduction, or modifications of published tests or parts thereof without the express permission and adequate recognition of the original author or publisher.

12. Regarding the preparation, publication, and distribution of tests, reference should be made to:

(a) *Standards for Educational and Psychological Tests and Manuals*, revised edition, 1973, published by the American Psychological Association on behalf of itself, the American Educational Research Association, and the National Council on Measurement in Education.

(b) "The Responsible Use of Tests: A Position Paper of AMEG, APGA, and NCME," published in *Measurement and Evaluation in Guidance*, Vol. 5, No. 2, July 1972, pp. 385-388.

Section D: Research and Publication

1. Current American Psychological Association guidelines on research with human subjects shall be adhered to (*Ethical Principles in the Conduct of Research with Human Participants*. Washington, D. C.: American Psychological Association, Inc., 1973).

2. In planning any research activity dealing with human subjects, the member is expected to be aware of and responsive to all pertinent ethical principles and to ensure that the research problem, design, and execution are in full compliance with them.

3. Responsibility for ethical research practice lies with the principal researcher, while others involved in the research activities share ethical obligation and full responsibility for their own actions.

4. In research with human subjects, researchers are responsible for their subjects' welfare throughout the experiment, and they must take all reasonable precautions to avoid causing injurious psychological, phsyical or social effects on their subjects.

5. It is expected that all research subjects be informed of the purpose of the study except when withholding information or providing misinformation to them is essential to the investigation. In such research, the member is responsible for corrective action as soon as possible following the research.

6. Participation in research is expected to be voluntary. Involuntary participation is appropriate only when it can be demonstrated that participation will have no harmful effects on subjects.

7.   When reporting research results, explicit mention must be made of all variables and conditions known to the investigator that might affect the outcome of the investigation or the interpretation of the data.

8.   The member is responsible for conducting and reporting investigations in a manner that minimizes the possibility that results will be misleading.

9.   The member has an obligation to make available sufficient original research data to qualified others who may wish to replicate the study.

10.   When supplying data, aiding in the research of another person, reporting research results, or in making original data available, due care must be taken to disguise the identity of the subjects in the absence of specific authorization from such subjects to do otherwise.

11.   When conducting and reporting research, the member is expected to be familiar with and to give recognition to previous work on the topic, as well as to observe all copyright laws and follow the principle of giving full credit to all of whom credit is due.

12.   The member has the obligation to give due credit through joint authorship, acknowledgement, footnote statements, or other appropriate means to those who have contributed significantly to the research, in accordance with such contributions.

13.   The member is expected to communicate to other members the results of any research judged to be of professional or scientific value. Results reflecting unfavorably on institutions, programs, services, or vested interests should not be withheld for such purposes.

14.   If members agree to cooperate with another individual in research and/or publication, they incur an obligation to cooperate as promised in terms of punctuality of performance and with full regard to the completeness and accuracy of the information provided.

Section E: **Consulting and Private Practice**

Consulting refers to a voluntary relationship between a professional helper and help-needing social unit (industry, business, school, college, etc.) in which the consultant is attempting to give help to the client in the solution of some current or potential problem. When "client" is used in this section it refers to an individual, group, or organization served by the consultant. (This definition of "consulting" is adapted from "Dimensions of the Consultant's Job", by Ronald Lippitt, *Journal of Social Issues*, Vol. 15, No. 2, 1959.

1.   Members who act as consultants must have a high degree of self-awareness of their own values and needs in entering helping relationships that involve change in social units.

2.   There should be understanding and agreement between consultant and client as to the task, the directions or goals, and the function of the consultant.

3.   Members are expected to accept only those consulting roles for which they possess or have access to the necessary skills and resources for giving the kind of help that is needed.

4.   The consulting relationship is defined as being one in which the client's adaptability and growth toward self-direction are encouraged and cultivated. For this reason, the consultant is obligated to maintain consistently the role of a consultant and to avoid becoming a decision maker for the client.

5.   In announcing one's availability for professional services as a consultant, the member follows professional rather than commercial standards in describing services with accuracy, dignity, and caution.

6.   For private practice in testing, counseling, or consulting, all ethical principles defined in this document are pertinent. In addition, any individual, agency, or institution offering educational, personal, or vocational counseling should meet the standards of the International Association of Counseling Services, Inc.

7.   The member is expected to refuse a private fee or other remuneration for consultation with persons who are entitled to these services through the member's employing institution or agency. The policies of a particular agency may make explicit provisions for private practice with agency counselees by members of its staff. In such instances, the counselees must be apprised of other options open to them should they seek private counseling services.

8.   It is unethical to use one's institutional affiliation to recruit counselees for one's private practice.

Section F: **Personnel Administration**

It is recognized that most members are employed in public or quasi-public institutions. The functioning of a member within an institution must contribute to the goals of the institution and vice versa if either is to accomplish their respective goals or objectives. It is therefore essential that the member and the institution function in ways to: (a) make the institution's goals explicit and public; (b) make the member's contribution to institutional goals specific; and (c) foster mutual accountability for goal achievement.

To accomplish these objectives it is recognized that the member and the employer must share responsibilities in the formulation and implementation of personnel policies.

1.   Members should define and describe the parameters and levels of their professional competency.

2.   Members should establish interpersonal relations and working agreements with supervisors and subordinates regarding counseling or clinical relationships, confidentiality, distinction between public and private material, maintenance and dissemination of recorded information, work load, and accountability. Working agreements in each instance should be specified and made known to those concerned.

3.   Members are responsible for alerting their employers to conditions that may be potentially disruptive or damaging.

4.   Members are responsible for informing employers of conditions that may limit their effectiveness.

5.   Members are expected to submit regularly to review and evaluation.

6.   Members are responsible for in-service development of self and/or staff.

7.   Members are responsible for informing their staff of goals and programs.

8.   Members are responsible for providing personnel practices that guarantee and enhance the rights and welfare of each recipient of their service.

9.   Members are expected to select competent persons and assign responsibilities compatible with their skills and experiences.

Section G: **Preparation Standards**

Members who are responsible for training others should be guided by the preparation standards of the Association and relevant division(s). The member who functions in the capacity of trainer assumes unique ethical responsibilities that frequently go beyond that of the member who does not function in a training capacity. These ethical responsibilities are outlined as follows:

1.   Members are expected to orient trainees to program expectations, basic skills development, and employment prospects prior to admission to the program.

2.   Members in charge of training are expected to establish programs that integrate academic study and supervised practice.

3.   Members are expected to establish a program directed toward developing the trainees' skills, knowledge, and self-understanding, stated whenever possible in competency or performance terms.

4.   Members are expected to identify the level of competency of their trainees. These levels of competency should accommodate the paraprofessional as well as the professional.

5.   Members, through continual trainee evaluation and appraisal, are expected to be aware of the personal limitations of the trainee that might impede future performance. The trainer has the responsibility of not only assisting the trainee in securing remedial assistance, but also screening from the program those trainees who are unable to provide competent services.

6.   Members are expected to provide a program that includes training in research commensurate with levels of role functioning. Paraprofessional and technician-level personnel should be trained as consumers of research. In addition, these personnel should learn how to evaluate their own and their program effectiveness. Advanced graduate training, especially at the doctoral level, should include preparation for original research by the member.

7.   Members are expected to make trainees aware of the ethical responsibilities and standards of the profession.

8.   Training programs are expected to encourage trainees to value the ideals of service to individuals and to society. In this regard, direct financial remuneration or lack thereof should not influence the quality of service rendered. Monetary considerations should not be allowed to overshadow professional and humanitarian needs.

9.   Members responsible for training are expected to be skilled as teachers and practitioners.

10.   Members are expected to present thoroughly varied theoretical positions so that trainees may make comparisons and have the opportunity to select a position.

11.   Members are obligated to develop clear policies within their training institution regarding field placement and the roles of the trainee and the trainer in such placements.

12.   Members are expected to ensure that forms of training focusing on self-understanding or growth are voluntary, or if required as part of the training program, are made known to prospective trainees prior to entering the program. When the training program offers a growth experience with an emphasis on self-disclosure or other relatively intimate or personal involvement, the member should have no administrative, supervisory, or evaluative authority regarding the participant.

13.   Members are obligated to conduct a training program in keeping with the most current guidelines of the American Personnel and Guidance Association and its various divisions.

Revised 1974
GUIDEPOST

APPENDIX B

AMERICAN PSYCHOLOGICAL ASSOCIATION

Ethical Standards of Psychologists[1]

PREAMBLE

Psychologists [2] respect the dignity and worth of the individual and honor the preservation and protection of fundamental human rights. They are committed to increasing knowledge of human behavior and of people's understanding of themselves and others and to the utilization of such knowledge for the promotion of human welfare. While pursuing these endeavors, they make every effort to protect the welfare of those who seek their services or of any human being or animal that may be the object of study. They use their skills only for purposes consistent with these values and do not knowingly permit their misuse by others. While demanding for themselves freedom of inquiry and communication, psychologists accept the responsibility this freedom requires: competence, objectivity in the application of skills and concern for the best interests of clients, colleagues, and society in general. In the pursuit of these ideals, psychologists subscribe to principles in the following areas: 1. Responsibility, 2. Competence, 3. Moral and Legal Standards, 4. Public Statements, 5. Confidentiality, 6. Welfare of the Consumer, 7. Professional Relationships, 8. Utilization of Assessment Techniques, and 9. Pursuit of Research Activities.

Principle One: RESPONSIBILITY

In their commitment to the understanding of human behavior, psychologists value objectivity and integrity, and in providing services they maintain the highest standards of their profession. They accept responsibility for the consequences of their work and make every effort to insure that their services are used appropriately.

a. As scientists, psychologists accept the ultimate responsibility for selecting appropriate areas and methods most relevant to these areas. They plan their research in ways to minimize the possibility that their findings will be misleading. They provide thorough discussion of the limitations of their data and alternative hypotheses, especially where their work touches on social policy or might be construed to the detriment of persons in specific age, sex, ethnic, socioeconomic or other social groups. In publishing reports of their work, they never suppress disconfirming data. Psychologists take credit only for the work they have actually done.

---

1 Approved by the Council of Representatives, January 30, 1977. Reprinted from the APA "Monitor," March 1977.

2 A student of psychology who asumes the role of a psychologist shall be considered a psychologist for the purpose of this code of ethics.

Psychologists clarify in advance with all appropriate persons or agencies the expectations for sharing and utilizing research data. They avoid dual relationships which may limit objectivity, whether political or monetary, so that interference with data, human participants, and milieu is kept to a minimum.

b.   As employees of an institution or agency, psychologists have the responsibility of remaining alert to and attempting to moderate institutional pressures that may distort reports of psychological findings or impede their proper use.

c.   As members of governmental or other organizational bodies, psychologists remain accountable as individuals to the highest standards of their profession.

d.   As teachers, psychologists recognize their primary obligation to help others acquire knowledge and skill. They maintain high standards of scholarship and objectivity by presenting psychological information fully and accurately.

e.   As practitioners, psychologists know that they bear a heavy social responsibility because their recommendations and professional actions may alter the lives of others. They are alert to personal, social, organizational, financial, or political situations or pressures that might lead to misuse of their influence.

f.   Psychologists provide adequate and timely evaluations to employees, trainees, students, and others whose work they supervise.

Principle Two: COMPETENCE

The maintenance of high standards of professional competence is a responsibility shared by all psychologists in the interest of the public and the profession as a whole. Psychologists recognize the boundaries of their competence and the limitations of their techniques and only provide services, use techniques, or offer opinions as professionals that meet recognized standards. Psychologists maintain knowledge of current scientific and professional information related to the services they render.

a.   Psychologists accurately represent their competence, education, training and experience. Psychologists claim as evidence of professional qualifications only those degrees obtained from institutions acceptable under the Bylaws and Rules of Council of the American Psychological Association.

b.   As teachers, psychologists perform their duties on the basis of careful preparation so that their instruction is accurate, current and scholarly.

c.   Psychologists recognize the need for continuing education and are open to new procedures and changes in expectations and values over time. They recognize differences among people, such as those that may be associated with age, sex, socioeconomic, and ethnic backgrounds. Where relevant, they obtain training, experience, or counsel to assure competent service or research relating to such persons.

d.   Psychologists with the responsibility for decisions involving individuals or policies based on test results have an understanding of psychological or educational measurement, validation problems and other test research.

e.   Psychologists recognize that their effectiveness depends in part upon their ability to maintain effective interpersonal relations, and that aberrations on their part may interfere with their abilities. They refrain from undertaking any activity in which their personal problems are likely to lead to inadequate professional services or harm to a client; or, if engaged in such activity when they become aware of their personal problems, they seek competent professional assistance to determine whether they should suspend, terminate or limit the scope of their professional and/or scientific activities.

Principle Three: MORAL AND LEGAL STANDARDS

Psychologists' moral, ethical and legal standards of behavior are a personal matter to the same degree as they are for any other citizen, except as these may compromise the fulfillment of their professional responsibilities, or reduce the trust in psychology or psychologists held by the general public. Regarding their own behavior, psychologists should be aware of the prevailing community standards and of the possible impact upon the quality of professional services provided by their conformity to or deviation from these standards. Psychologists are also aware of the possible impact of their public behavior upon the ability of colleagues to perform their professional duties.

a.   Psychologists as teachers are aware of the diverse backgrounds of students and, when dealing with topics that may give offense, treat the material objectively and present it in a manner for which the student is prepared.

b.   As employees, psychologists refuse to participate in practices inconsistent with legal, moral and ethical standards regarding the treatment of employees or of the public. For example, psychologists will not condone practices that are inhumane or that result in illegal or otherwise unjustifiable discrimination on the basis of race, age, sex, religion, or national origin in hiring, promotion, or training.

c.   In providing psychological services, psychologists avoid any action that will violate or diminish the legal and civil rights of clients or of others who may be affected by their actions.

As practitioners, psychologists remain abreast of relevant federal, state, local, and agency regulations and Association standards of practice concerning the conduct of their practice. They are concerned with developing such legal and quasi-legal regulations as best serve the public interest and in changing such existing regulations as are not beneficial to the interests of the public and the profession.

d.   As researchers, psychologists remain abreast of relevant federal and state regulations concerning the conduct of research with human participants or animals.

Principle Four: PUBLIC STATEMENTS

Public statements, announcements of services, and promotional activities of psychologists serve the purpose of providing sufficient information to aid the consumer public in making informed judgments and choices. Psychologists represent accurately and objectively their professional qualifications, affiliations, and functions, as well as those of the institutions or organizations with which they or the statements may be associated. In public statements providing psychological information or professional opinions or providing information about the availability of psychological products and services, psychologists take full account of the limits and uncertainties of present psychological knowlege and techniques.

      a.   When announcing professional services, psychologists limit the information to: name, highest academic degree conferred, date and type of certification or licensure, diplomate status, address, telephone number, office hours, and, at the individual practitioner's discretion, an appropriate brief listing of the types of psychological services offered, and fee information. Such statements are descriptive of services provided but not evaluative as to their quality or uniqueness. They do not contain testimonials by quotation or by implication. They do not claim uniqueness of skills or methods unless determined by acceptable and public scientific evidence.

      b.   In announcing the availability of psychological services or products, psychologists do not display any affiliations with an organization in a manner that falsely implies the sponsorship or certification of that organization. In particular and for example psychologists do not offer APA membership or fellowship as evidence of qualification. They do not name their employer or professional associations unless the services are in fact to be provided by or under the responsible, direct supervision and continuing control of such organizations or agencies.

      c.   Announcements of "personal growth groups" give a clear statement of purpose and the nature of the experiences to be provided. The education, training and experience of the psychologists are appropriately specified.

      d.   Psychologists associated with the development or promotion of psychological devices, books, or other products offered for commercial sale make every effort to insure that announcements and advertisements are presented in a professional, scientifically acceptable, and factually informative manner.

      e.   Psychologists do not participate for personal gain in commercial announcements recommending to the general public the purchase or use of any proprietary or single-source product or service.

      f.   Psychologists who interpret the science of psychology or the services of psychologists to the general public accept the obligation to present the material fairly and accurately, avoiding misrepresentation through sensationalism, exaggeration or superficiality. Psychologists are guided by the primary obligation to aid the public in forming their own informed judgments, opinions and choices.

      g.   As teachers, psychologists insure that statements in catalogs and course outlines are accurate and sufficient, particularly in terms of subject matter to be covered, bases for evaluating progress, and nature of course experiences. Announcements or brochures describing workshops, seminars, or other education programs accurately represent intended audience and eligibility requirements, educational objectives, and nature of the material to be covered, as well as the education, training and experience of the psychologists presenting the programs, and any fees involved. Public announcements soliciting subjects for research, and in which clinical services or other professional services are offered as an inducement, make clear the nature of the services as well as the costs and other obligations to be accepted by the human participants of the research.

h.   Psychologists accept the obligation to correct others who may represent the psychologist's professional qualifications or associations with products or services in a manner incompatible with these guidelines.

i.   Psychological services for the purposes of diagnosis, treatment or personal advice are provided only in the context of a professional relationship, and are not given by means of public lectures or demonstrations, newspaper or magazine articles, radio or television programs, mail, or similar media.

Principle Five: CONFIDENTIALITY

Safeguarding information about an individual that has been obtained by the psychologist in the course of his teaching, practice, or investigation is a primary obligation of the psychologist. Such information is not communicated to others unless certain important conditions are not met.

a.   Information received in confidence is revealed only after most careful deliberation and when there is clear and imminent danger to an individual or to society, and then only to appropriate professional workers or public authorities.

b.   Information obtained in clinical or consulting relationships, or evaluative data concerning children, students, employees, and others are discussed only for professional purposes and only with persons clearly concerned with the case. Written and oral reports should present only data germane to the purposes of the evaluation and every effort should be made to avoid undue invasion of privacy.

c.   Clinical and other materials are used in classroom teaching and writing only when the identity of the persons involved is adequately disguised.

d.   The confidentiality of professional communications about individuals is maintained. Only when the originator and other persons involved give their express permission is a confidential professional communication shown to the individual concerned. The psychologist is responsible for informing the client of the limits of the confidentiality.

e.   Only after explicit permission has been granted is the identity of research subjects published. When data have been published without permission for identification, the psychologist assumes responsibility for adequately disguising their sources.

f.   The psychologist makes provisions for the maintenance of confidentiality in the prevention and ultimate disposition of confidential records.

Principle Six: WELFARE OF THE CONSUMER

Psychologists respect the integrity and protect the welfare of the people and groups with whom they work. When there is a conflict of interest between the client and the psychologist's employing institution, psychologists clarify the nature and direction of their loyalties and responsibilities and keep all parties informed of their commitments. Psychologists fully inform consumers as to the purpose and nature of an evaluative, treatment, educational or training procedure, and they freely acknowledge that clients, students, or participants in research have freedom of choice with regard to participation.

a.   Psychologists are continually cognizant of their own needs and of their inherently powerful position vis a vis clients, in order to avoid exploiting their trust and dependency. Psychologists make every effort to avoid dual relationships with clients and/or relationships which might impair their professional judgment or increase the risk of client exploitation. Examples of such dual relationships include treating employees, supervisors, close friends or relatives. Sexual intimacies with clients are unethical.

b.   Where demands of an organization of psychologists go beyond reasonable conditions of employment, psychologists recognize possible conflicts of interest that may arise. When such conflicts occur, psychologists clarify the nature of the conflict and inform all parties of the nature and direction of the loyalties and responsibilities involved.

c.   When acting as a supervisor, trainer, researcher, or employer, psychologists accord informed choice, confidentiality, due process, and protection from physical and mental harm to their subordinates in such relationships.

d.   Financial arrangements in professional practice are in accord with professional standards that safeguard the best interests of the client and that are clearly understood by the client in advance of billing. Psychologists are responsible for assisting clients in finding needed services in those instances where payment of the usual fee would be a hardship. No commission, rebate, or other form of remuneration may be given or received for referral of clients for professional services, whether by an individual or by an agency. Psychologists willingly contribute a portion of their services to work for which they receive little or no financial return.

e.   The psychologist attempts to terminate a clinical or consulting relationship when it is reasonably clear that the consumer is not benefiting from it. Psychologists who find that their services are being used by employers in a way that is not beneficial to the participants or to employees who may be affected, or to significant others, have the responsibility to make their observations known to the responsible persons and to propose modification or termination of the engagement.

Principle Seven: PROFESSIONAL RELATIONSHIPS

Psychologists act with due regard for the needs, special competencies and obligations of their colleagues in psychology and other professions. Psychologists respect the prerogatives and obligations of the institutions or organizations with which they are associated.

a.   Psychologists understand the areas of competence of related professions, and make full use of all the professional, technical, and administrative resources that best serve the interests of consumers. The absence of formal relationships with other professional co-workers does not relieve psychologists from the responsibility of securing for their clients the best possible professional service nor does it relieve them from the exercise of foresight, diligence, and tact in obtaining the complementary or alternative assistance needed by clients.

b.   Psychologists know and take into account the traditions and practices of other professional groups with which they work and cooperate fully with members of such groups. If a consumer is receiving services from another professional, psychologists do not offer their services directly to the consumer without first informing the professional person already involved so that the risk of confusion and conflict for the consumer can be avoided.

c.   Psychologists who employ or supervise other professionals or professionals in training accept the obligation to facilitate their further professional development by providing suitable working conditions, consultation, and experience opportunities.

d.   As employees of organizations providing psychological services, or as independent psychologists serving clients in an organizational context, psychologists seek to support the integrity, reputation and proprietary rights of the host organization. When it is judged necessary in a client's interest to question the organization's programs or policies, psychologists attempt to effect change by constructive action within the organization before disclosing confidential information acquired in their professional roles.

e.   In the pursuit of research, psychologists give sponsoring agencies, host institutions, and publication channels the same respect and opportunity for giving informed consent that they accord to individual research participants. They are aware of their obligation to future research workers and insure that host institutions are given adequate information about the research and proper acknowledgement of their contributions.

f.   Publication credit is assigned to all those who have contributed to a publication in proportion to their contribution. Major contributions of a professional character made by several persons to a common project are recognized by joint authorship, with the experimenter or author who made the principal contribution identified and listed first. Minor contributions of a professional character, extensive clerical or similar nonprofessional assistance, and other minor contributions are acknowledged in footnotes or in an introductory statement. Acknowledgement through specific citations is made for unpublished as well as published material that has directly influenced the research or writing. A psychologist who compiles and edits material of others for publication publishes the material in the name of the originating group, if any, and with his/her own name appearing as chairperson or editor. All contributors are to be acknowledged and named.

g.   When a psychologist violates ethical standards, psychologists who know first-hand of such activities should, if possible, attempt to rectify the situation. Failing an informal solution, psychologists bring such unethical activities to the attention of the appropriate local, state, and/or national committee on professional ethics, standards, and practices.

h.   Members of the Association cooperate with duly constituted committees of the Association, in particular and for example, the Committee on Scientific and Professional Ethics and Conduct, and the Committee on Professional Standards Review, by responding to inquiries promptly and completely. Members taking longer than thirty days to respond to such inquiries shall have the burden of demonstrating that they acted with "reasonable promptness." Members also have a similar responsibility to respond with reasonable promptness to inquiries from duly constituted state association ethics committees and professional standards review committees.

Principle Eight: UTILIZATION OF ASSESSMENT TECHNIQUES

In the development, publication, and utilization of psychological assessment techniques, psychologists observe relevant APA standards. Persons examined have the right to know the results, the interpretations made, and, when appropriate, the original data on which final judgments were based. Test users avoid imparting unnecessary information which would compromise test security, but they provide required information that explains the basis for decisions that may adversely affect that person or that person's dependents.

a.   The client has the right to have and the psychologist has the responsibility to provide explanations of the nature and the purposes of the test and the test results in language that the client can understand, unless, as in some employment or school settings, there is an explicit exception to this right agreed upon in advance. When the explanations are to be provided by others, the psychologist establishes procedures for providing adequate explanations.

b.   When a test is published or otherwise made available for operational use, it is accompanied by a manual (or other published or readily available information) that fully describes the development of the test, the rationale, and evidence of validity and reliability. The test manual explicitly states the purposes and applications for which the test is recommended and identifies special qualifications required to administer the test and to interpret it properly. Test manuals provide complete information regarding characteristics of the normative population.

c.   In reporting test results, psychologists indicate any reservations regarding validity or reliability resulting from testing circumstances or inappropriateness of the test norms for the person tested. Psychologists strive to insure that the test results and their interpretations are not misused by others.

d.   Psychologists accept responsibility for removing from clients' files test score information that has become obsolete, lest such information be misused or misconstrued to the disadvantage of the person tested.

e.   Psychologists offering test scoring and interpretation services are able to demonstrate that the validity of the programs and procedures used in arriving at interpretations are based on appropriate evidence. The public offering of an automated test interpretation service is considered as a professional-to-professional consultation. The psychologist makes every effort to avoid misuse of test reports.

Principle Nine: PURSUIT OF RESEARCH ACTIVITIES

The decision to undertake research should rest upon a considered judgment by the individual psychologist about how best to contribute to psychological science and to human welfare. Psychologists carry out their investigations with respect for the people who participate and with concern for their dignity and welfare.

a.   In planning a study the investigator has the responsibility to make a careful evaluation of its ethical acceptability, taking into account the following additional principles for research with human beings. To the extent that this appraisal, weighing scientific and human values, suggests a compromise of any principle, the investigator incurs an increasingly serious obligation to seek ethical advice and to observe stringent safeguards to protect the rights of the human research participants.

b.   Responsibility for the establishment and maintenance of acceptable ethical practice in research always remains with the individual investigator. The investigator is also responsible for the ethical treatment of research participants by collaborators, assistants, students, and employees, all of whom, however, incur parallel obligations.

c.   Ethical practice requires the investigator to inform the participant of all features of the research that might reasonably be expected to influence willingness to participate, and to explain all other aspects of the research about which the participant inquires. Failure to make full disclosure imposes additional force to the investigator's abiding responsibility to protect the welfare and dignity of the research participant.

d.   Openness and honesty are essential characteristics of the relationship between investigator and research participant. When the methodological requirements of a study necessitate concealment or deception, the investigator is required to insure as soon as possible the participant's understanding of the reasons for this action and of a sufficient justification for the procedures employed.

e.   Ethical practice requires the investigator to respect the individual's freedom to decline to participate in or withdraw from research. The obligation to protect this freedom requires special vigilance when the investigator is in a position of power over the participant, as, for example, when the participant is a student, client, employee, or otherwise is in a dual relationship with the investigator.

f.   Ethically acceptable research begins with the establishment of a clear and fair agreement between the investigator and the research participant that clarifies the responsibilities of each. The investigator has the obligation to honor all promises and commitments included in that agreement.

g.   The ethical investigator protects participants from physical and mental discomfort, harm, and danger. If a risk of such consequences exists, the investigator, is required to inform the participant of that fact, secure consent before proceeding, and take all possible measures to minimize distress. A research procedure must not be used if it is likely to cause serious or lasting harm to a participant.

h.   After the data are collected, the investigator provides the participant with information about the nature of the study and to remove any misconceptions that might have arisen. When scientific or human values justify delaying or withholding information, the investigator acquires a special responsibility to assure that there are no damaging consequences for the participant.

i.   When research procedures may result in undesirable consequences for the individual participant, the investigator has the responsibility to detect and remove or correct these consequences, including where relevant, long-term after effects.

j.   Information obtained about the individual research participants during the course of an investigation is confidential unless otherwise agreed in advance. When the possibility exists that others may obtain access to such information, this possibility, together with the plans for protecting confidentiality, be explained to the participants as part of the procedure for obtaining informed consent.

k.   A psychologist using animals in research adheres to the provisions of the Rules Regarding Animals, drawn up by the Committee on Precautions and Standards in Animal Experimentation and adopted by the American Psychological Association.

l.   Investigations of human participants using drugs should be conducted only in such settings as clinics, hospitals, or research facilities maintaining appropriate safeguards for the participants.

REFERENCES

Psychologists are responsible for knowing about and acting in accord with the standards and positions of the APA, as represented in such official documents as the following:

American Association of University Professors. Statement on Principles on Academic Freedom and Tenure. *Policy Documents & Report*, 1966, 1-4.

American Psychological Association. *Guidelines for Psychologists for the Use of Drugs in Research*. Washington, D. C.: Author, 1971.

American Psychological Association. *Principles for the Care and Use of Animals*. Washington, D. C.: Author, 1971.

American Psychological Association. Guidelines for conditions of employment of psychologists. *American Psychologist*, 1972, *27*, 331-334.

American Psychological Association. Guidelines for psychologists conducting growth groups. *American Psychologist*, 1973, *28*, 933.

American Psychological Association. *Ethical Principles in the Conduct of Research with Human Participants*. Washington, D. C.: Author, 1973.

American Psychological Association. *Standards for Educational and Psychological Tests*. Washington, D. C.: Author, 1974.

American Psychological Association. *Standards for Providers of Psychological Services*. Washington, D. C.: Author, 1977.

Committee on Scientific and Professional Ethics and Conduct. Guidelines for telephone directory listings. *American Psychologist*, 1969, *24*, 70-71.

Abelson, R. & Friquegnon, M. *Ethics for modern life.* New York: St. Martin's Press, 1975.

Adler, A. *Understanding human nature.* New York: Fawcett, 1954.

Allan, D. J. *The philosophy of Aristotle.* (2nd ed.) London: Oxford University Press, 1970.

American Personnel and Guidance Association, Ethical Practices Committee. *Ethical standards casebook.* Washington, D. C., 1965.

American Personnel and Guidance Association. *Ethical standards.* Washington, D. C., 1974.

American Psychological Association. *Ethical standards of psychologists.* Washington, D. C., 1977.

American Psychiatric Association. *The principles of medical ethics.* Washington, D. C., 1973.

Arbuckle, D. S. *Counseling: Philosophy, theory, and practice.* Boston: Allyn & Bacon, 1965.

Baldwin, J. M. *Social and ethical interpretation in mental development.* New York: Macmillan, 1906.

Barchilon, J. *Malpractice and you.* New York: Ace Books, 1975.

Beck, C. E. Ethical practices: Foundations and emerging issues. *Personnel and Guidance Journal,* 1971, *50,* 320-325.

Benjamin, A. *The helping interview.* Boston: Houghton Mifflin, 1974.

Bentham, J. An introduction to the principles and morals of legislation. In R. B. Brandt (Ed.), *Value and obligation.* New York: Harcourt, Brace & World, 1961.

Blatt, M. & Kohlberg, L. Effects of classroom discussion upon children's level of moral judgment. In L. Kohlberg (Ed.), *Recent research in moral development.* New York: Holt, Rinehart and Winston, in press.

Boyd, R. E., Tennyson, W. W. & Erikson, R. Changes in counselor disclosure of data from 1962 to 1970. *Measurement and Evaluation in Guidance,* 1974, *7,* 32-38.

Boyd, R. E., Tennyson, W. W. & Erikson, R. Counselor and client confidentiality. *Counselor Education and Supervision,* 1973, *12,* 278-288.

Brandt, R. B. (Ed.) *Value and obligation.* New York: Harcourt, Brace & World, 1961.

Browne, H. *How I found freedom in an unfree world.* New York: Avon Books, 1973.

Buhler, C. *Values in psychotherapy.* New York: The Free Press, 1962.

Burton, R. V. Generality of honesty reconsidered. *Psychological Review,* 1963, *70,* 481-499.

Carkhuff, R. R. *The art of problem-solving.* Amherst, Massachusetts: Human Resource Development Press, 1973.

Cooper, J. *The new mentality.* Philadelphia: Westminster Press, 1969.

Cramer, S. H., Groff, R. & Zani, L. P. Counselor recommendations of typical students. *Vocational Guidance Quarterly,* 1969, *18,* 119-122.

Daubner, E. V. & Daubner, E. S. Ethics and counselor decisions. *Personnel and Guidance Journal*, 1970, *48*, 433-442.

Dewey, J. What psychology can do for the teacher. In R. Archambault (Ed.), *John Dewey on education: Selected writings*. New York: Random House, 1964.

Dorken, H. and associates. *The professional psychologist today*. San Francisco: Jossey-Bass, Inc., 1976.

Dunham, B. *Ethics dead and alive*. New York: Knopf, 1971.

Fish, J. *Placebo therapy: A practical guide to social influence in psychotherapy*. San Francisco: Jossey-Bass, Inc., 1973.

Fromm, E. *Man for himself: An inquiry into the psychology of ethics*. Greenwich, Connecticut: Fawcett, 1974.

Gelatt, H. B. Decision-making: A conceptual frame of reference for counseling. *Journal of Counseling Psychology*, 1962, *9* (3), 240-245.

Goslin, D. A. Ethical and legal aspects of school record keeping. *NASSP*, 1971, *55*, 119-126.

Grossback, M. & Gardner, H. *Man and men*. Scranton, Penn.: International Textbook Co., 1972.

Hartshorne, H. & May, M. A. *Studies in deceit*. New York: Macmillan, 1928.

Hartshorne, H. & May, M. A. *Studies in the organization of character*. New York, 1930.

Heilman, M. E., Hodgson, S. A. & Hornstein, H. A. Effects of magnitude and rectifiability of harm and information value on reporting of accidental harm-doing. *Journal of Personality and Social Psychology*, 1972, *23*, 211-218.

Hetherington, E. M. & Feldman, S. E. College cheating as a function of subject and situational variables. *Journal of Educational Psychology*, 1964, *55*, 212-218.

Hobhouse, L. *Morals in evolution*. London: Chapman and Hall, 1906.

Johnson, O. A. (Ed.) *Ethics: Selections from classical and contemporary writers*. (3rd ed.) New York: Holt, Rinehart and Winston, 1974.

Jones, W. T., Sontag, F., Beckner, M. & Fogelin, R. *Approaches to ethics*. (2nd ed.) New York: McGraw-Hill, 1969.

Jung, C. G. *Man and his symbols*. New York: Doubleday, 1964.

Kaplan, P. S. Counselor ethics and the faculty. *School Counselor*, 1974, *21*, 232-235.

Kemp, C. *Intangibles in counseling*. Boston: Houghton Mifflin, 1967.

Kohlberg, L. The cognitive developmental approach to moral education. *Phi Delta Kappan*, 1975, *56* (10), 670-677.

Kohlberg, L. From is to ought. In T. Mischel (Ed.), *Cognitive development and epistomology*. New York: Academic Press, 1971 (a).

Kohlberg, L. Moral development and education of adolescents. In R. Purnell (Ed.), *Adolescents and the American high school*. New York: Holt, Rinehart, & Winston, 1971 (b).

Kohlberg, L. Education for justice. In N. F. Sizer and T. R. Sizer (Eds.), *Moral education*. Cambridge, Mass.: Harvard University Press, 1970.

Kohlberg, L. Moral stages and moralization. In T. Lickona (Ed.), *Moral development and behavior*. New York: Holt, Rinehart & Winston, 1976.

Krumboltz, J. D. & Thoresen, C. *Counseling methods*. New York: Holt, Rinehart and Winston, 1976.

London, P. *The modes and morals of psychotherapy*. New York: Holt, Rinehart and Winston, 1976.

Lowe, M. *Value orientations in counseling and psychotherapy*. (2nd Ed.) Cranston, R. I.: The Carroll Press, 1976.

May, M. A. Mark A. May talks on the Character Education Inquiry. Cited by W. W. May, A psychologist of many hats: A tribute to Mark Arthur May. *American Psychologist*, 1978, *33*(7), 653-663.

May, R. *Psychology and the human dilemma*. New York: Van Nostrand, 1967.

May, R. *Man's search for himself*. New York: W. W. Norton, 1953.

Maslow, A. H. Deficiency motivation and growth motivation. In M. R. Jones (Ed.), *Nebraska symposium on motivation*. Lincoln: University of Nebraska Press, 1955.

Maslow, A. H. *Toward a psychology of being*. (2nd Ed.) Princeton: Van Nostrand, 1968.

Mill, J. S. Utilitarianism. In R. B. Brandt (Ed.), *Value and obligation*. New York: Harcourt, Brace, & World, 1961.

Mischel, W. & Mischel, H. A cognitive social-learning approach to morality and self-regulation. In T. Lickona (Ed.), *Moral development and behavior*. New York: Holt, Rinehart, and Winston, 1976.

Moore, G. E. *Principa ethica*. Cambridge: University Press, 1971.

Moore, G. E. *Ethics*. London: Oxford University Press, 1969.

McDougall, W. *An introduction to social psychology*. London: Methuen, 1908.

Nelson, E. A., Grinder, R. E. & Mutterer, M. S. Sources of variance in behavioral measures of honesty in temptation situations. *Developmental Psychology*, 1969, *1*, 265-279.

Nugent, F. A. Confidentiality in college counseling centers. *Personnel and Guidance Journal*, 1969, *47*, 872-877.

Paradise, L. V. What price ethics: New research directions in counselor ethical behavior. *Counseling and Values*, 1978, *23* (1) 2-9.

Paradise, L. V. Toward a theory on the ethical behavior of counselors. Unpublished doctoral dissertation. University of Virginia, 1976.

Perry, R. B. General theory of value. In O. A. Johnson (Ed.), *Ethics: Selections from classical and contemporary writers*. (3rd Ed.) New York: Holt, Rinehart and Winston, 1974.

Peterson, J. *Counseling and values*. Cranston, R. I.: The Carroll Press, 1976.

Piaget, J. *Judgment and reasoning in the child*. New York: Harcourt, 1926.

Piaget, J. *The moral judgment of the child*. New York: Free Press, 1965.

Rackham, H. (Trans.) *Aristotle, ethics for English readers*. Oxford: Basil Blackwell Publishing, 1952.

Reisman, D. et al. *The lonely crowd*. New York: Doubleday, 1950.

Rest, J., Turiel, E. & Kohlberg, L. Relations between level of moral judgment and preference and comprehension of the moral judgment of others. *Journal of Personality*, 1969, *37*, 225-252.

Ritchie, M. The professional status of counseling. Unpublished doctoral dissertation. University of Virginia, 1978.

Rogers, C. R. *Counseling and psychotherapy*. Boston: Houghton Mifflin, 1942.

Rogers, C. R. *Client-centered therapy*. Boston: Houghton Mifflin, 1951.

Rogers, C. R. *On becoming a person*. Boston: Houghton Mifflin, 1961.

Rogers, C. R. Toward a modern approach to values. In M. Bloomberg (Ed.), *Creativity: Theory and research*. New Haven: College and University Press, 1972.

Ross, W. D. What makes right acts right? In K. Pahel and M. Schiller (Eds.), *Readings in contemporary ethical theory*. Englewood Cliffs, N. J.: Prentice-Hall, Inc., 1970.

Rudolph, J. T. Questions related to the release of student personnel information. *School Counselor*, 1968, *16*, 108-114.

Russell, B. *Wisdom of the west*. London: Rathbone Books, 1959.

Schwebel, M. Why unethical practice? *Journal of Counseling Psychology*, 1955, *2*, 122-128.

Sears, R. R., Rau, L. & Alpert, R. *Identification in child rearing*. Stanford, California: Stanford University Press, 1965.

Shertzer, B. & Morris K. APGA members' ethical discrimination ability. *Counselor Education and Supervision*, 1972, *11*, 200-206.

Sidgwick, H. Ethical judgments. In R. B. Brandt (Ed.), *Value and obligation*. New York: Harcourt, Brace, & World, 1961.

Smith, C. E. Development of ethical standards in the secondary school counseling relationship for the use of counseling information. Unpublished doctoral dissertation. University of Southern California, 1956. (Abstract)

Snygg, D. The psychological basis of human values. In D. Anila, A. Combs and W. Purkey (Eds.), *The helping relationship source book*. Boston: Allyn and Bacon, 1972.

Swanson, C. & Van Hoose, W. *Legal and ethical concerns of school counselors*. Athens, Georgia: Department of Education, 1976.

Tolbert, E. L. *Counseling for career development*. Boston: Houghton Mifflin, 1974.

Toulmin, S. *Reason in ethics*. London: Cambridge University Press, 1968.

Turiel, E. An experimental test of the sequentiality of development stages in the child's moral judgments. *Journal of Personality and Social Psychology*, 1966, *3*(6), 611-618.

Vafakas, K. M.   Ethical behavior of community college students. *Journal of College Student Personnel*, 1974, *15*(2), 101-104.

Van Hoose, W. H. & Paradise, L. V.   On the ethical behavior of counselors. Paper presented to the Annual Convention of the American Personnel and Guidance Association, Dallas, March, 1977.

Van Hoose, W. H. & Goldman, C.   Some ethical dilemmas of the helping professions. Unpublished report, Wayne State University, 1971. (Mimeographed)

Van Hoose, W. H. & Kottler, J.   *Ethical and legal issues in counseling and psychotherapy*. San Francisco: Jossey-Bass, 1977.

Ware, M. L.   The law and counselor ethics. *Personnel and Guidance Journal*, 1971, *50*, 305-311.

Whyte, W.   *The organization man*. New York: Doubleday, 1956.

Williams, R.   *American society*. New York: Knopf, 1956.

Wiskoff, M.   Ethical standards and divided loyalties. *American Psychologist*, 1960, *15*, 656-660.

SUBJECT INDEX

AUTHOR INDEX

THE ETHICAL JUDGMENT SCALE

MANUAL

by

Louis V. Paradise, Ph.D.
Catholic University of America

and

William H. Van Hoose, Ph.D.
University of Virginia

PREFACE

This manual describes the development of the Ethical Judgment Scale (EJS), discusses the rationale for the scale, and provides information on its use in research and in the training of counselors and psychotherapists using the ethical decision making process.

Originally designed primarily as a research instrument, we have found increasing use for the EJS in the training of helping professionals using ethical awareness. This revised version reflects certain changes that have occurred in our original thinking and also incorporates data gleaned from its use with over 500 people in training and in research at Wayne State University, The University of Virginia, and at Catholic University of America during the period 1971-1978.

We would hope that the EJS would stimulate continued research on ethical behavior as well as provide a training vehicle which counselors and other helping professionals could use to gain a greater awareness of their ethical orientations.

LOUIS V. PARADISE
WILLIAM H. VAN HOOSE

Introduction

The *Ethical Judgment Scale* (EJS) is a measure used to assess the ethical orientation of counselors. It is based on the theoretical formulations of counselor ethical development initially proposed by Van Hoose (1971) with later theoretical additions by Van Hoose and Paradise (1977) and Paradise (1976).

The initial development of the scale was completed with a sample of twenty-four students in a counselor training program at Wayne State University. Later, Van Hoose and Goldman (1971) used the scale as an investigation of the ethical behavior of school counselors and school social workers with encouraging success. Further research and development of the scale were conducted by Vafakas (1972, 1974) in a study of the ethical posture of community college counselors in Michigan. Additional work related to the theoretical formulations associated with measurement instrument was completed by Paradise (1976) at the University of Virginia using advanced counseling students.

Reliability and validity data reported in this manual are based upon the initial research reported by Vafakas (1972) and Paradise (1976). At that time the EJS contained fifteen stimulus vignettes. Based upon past research and development, the scale was modified and extended to contain twenty-five vignettes encompassing a greater scope and range of ethical dilemmas facing the helping professions. It was the authors' desire to not only improve the research potential of the scale, but also to develop an instrument which would serve as a vehicle for the ethical training and development of helping professionals. It is believed that the modifications and revisions made to the initial scale not only improve its psychometric properties, but also greatly enhance its potential as an ethical training technique. Presently, with no other materials or scales addressing ethical issues, it is our belief that the EJS can contribute to a greater individual awareness of ethical behavior in terms of research and training in this critical area of concern.

The Ethical Orientation of Counselors

Concern for the ethical behavior of counselors is an area of increasing importance. The focus of the concern is not only demonstrated by emphasis on ethical codification, but also on the actual ethical behavior of practicing counselors (Paradise, 1978). Therefore, the ethical training and development of the practitioner becomes a critical area of inquiry for the profession. As such, its theoretical neglect is obvious. Our purpose in this manual is to provide a theoretical conceptualization together with a systematic assessment and training procedure to investigate and explore ethical orientation.

In attempting to structure a theoretical framework from which to examine the development of ethical behavior, the authors were greatly influenced by the work of moral developmentalists such as Dewey, Piaget, and Kohlberg. It was felt that significant analogues from moral development theory (Dewey, 1964; Kohlberg, 1963, 1975; Piaget, 1965), could be translated into an effective approach for examining the ethical behavior of counselors. In view of this, it was postulated that the ethical orientation of counselors, that is, the rationale underlying individual ethical decision-making, could be viewed from a model of five, qualitatively different stages of orientation, increasing through discernably different levels of ethical reasoning. For a more complete discussion of the relationship of ethical orientation to the moral developmentalist position, see Van Hoose and Paradise (1979), *Ethics in Counseling and Psychotherapy*.

The stages of ethical behavior are conceptualized as follows:

>   *Stage I.* **Punishment Orientation**: Counselor decisions, suggestions and courses of action are based on a strict adherence to prevailing rules and standards, i. e., one must be punished for bad behavior and rewarded for good behavior. The primary concern is the strict attention to the physical consequences of the decision.

>   *Stage II.* **Institutional Orientation**: Counselor decisions, suggestions and courses of action are based on a strict adherence to the rules and policies of the institution or agency. The correct posture is based upon the expectations of higher authorities.

>   *Stage III.* **Societal Orientation**: The maintenance of standards, approval of others, and the laws of society and the general public characterize this stage of ethical behavior. Concern is for duty and societal welfare.

>   *Stage IV.* **Individual Orientation**: The primary concern of the counselor is for the needs of the individual while avoiding the violation of laws and the rights of others. Concern for law and societal welfare is recognized, but is secondary to the needs of the individual.

>   *Stage V.* **Principle or Conscience Orientation**: Concern is for the legal, professional, or societal consequences. What is right, in accord with self-chosen principles of conscience and internal ethical formulations, determines counselor behavior.

Within this stage of ethical behavior, it is assumed that most counselors do not function solely at any given level, and that those varying levels are also a function of other related variables, such as situational factors, training, etc. Thus, the EJS is an attempt at inquiry into the reasoning process which underlies decisions resulting from ethical dilemmas .

The proposed ethical orientations not only describe qualitatively discrete stages, but reflect an underlying continuum of ethical reasoning from which the bases of ethical judgments are made. A closer examination of the proposed ethical orientations will demonstrate this.

Stage I, the punishment orientation, is an ethical orientation totally dependent upon external rationale. Right and wrong are defined totally by the punishments and rewards that are viewed as present in the environment. Counselors functioning at this orientation are governed by prevailing sanctions and the physical consequences of the behavior involved. When faced with ethical dilemmas, decisions become fundamental and absolute for the counselor.

Stage II, the institutional orientation, in which adherence is to the institutional rules and policies, is to a lesser degree another example of an external modality of reasoning. The counselor functioning at this level needs only to look to his/her organization's operating procedures and policies to determine appropriate ethical conduct when faced with a dilemma. There is little room for conflict with expectations from higher authorities.

Stage III, the societal orientation, reflects the concern of the counselor with duty and societal welfare, not the individual. Thus, there is less external emphasis regarding the modality of reasoning than in the previous stage. But, nonetheless, the judgment as to right and wrong behaviors is derived essentially from an external source.

Stage IV, the individual orientation, reflects ethical judgments more internally-controlled than in previous stages, with concern for the needs and worth of the individual. The welfare of society and the institution are recognized, but are clearly secondary to the needs of the individual. The counselor at this level of orientation, when faced with an ethical dilemma, considers the individual the primary concern with the rationale for decisions reflecting this focus.

Stage V, the principle orientation, is the highest level of reasoning, reflecting a totally internal modality. The individual is primary with little regard for legal, professional, and societal consequences. Right is defined by a decision of conscience in agreement with one's own defined internal ethical system. A counselor with this orientation, when faced with an ethical dilemma, reflects on his/her own principles of conduct, without regard for external consequences. At this level, the consequences of concern to the counselor are all internally based.

Counselors do not adhere passively to external norms nor to ethical codes without assessing the relevance to their own personal system of ethical principles.

Considering this implied continuum of ethical judgment that is described, the notion that some ethical judgments are more adequate than others appears to be a safe assumption. One counselor may function primarily within a given stage across more situations, and in a more appropriate manner than another counselor. However, the relevance at this point in the development of a useful theory on ethical behavior lies mainly in its qualitative aspect, not its quantitative aspect. We are more concerned with describing the functioning ethical orientation of counselors as a method for exploring the issue, rather than saying that one counselor is more ethical than another, from a purely quantitative aspect.

However, it should be reemphasized that Stage V reasoning can be viewed as a more appropriate ethical posture because it is based upon universal principles on which all moral individuals can agree. When the rationale for an ethical decision is based upon conventional rules, such as those of society or an institution, disagreement due to cultural and social differences is likely to ensue. Ethical resolutions, based upon internal principles of human conduct, transcend this disagreement and, in that sense, are "better" than those of a lower stage orientation.

In summary, the ethical orientation stages not only describe qualitatively discrete stages, but reflect to a certain extent, an underlying continuum of ethical reasoning. Awareness and examination of the rationale and reasoning function for the self-development of the counselor.

How to Score the Ethical Judgment Scale

The Ethical Judgment Scale contains twenty-five hypothetical case incidents or problems that may confront a counselor or therapist in his or her work with clients. Respondents are asked to select, from five responses, the alternative that best describes the decision they would make in dealing with the case. Also, space is provided for the respondent to briefly describe why a given alternative was chosen. Thus the stage of ethical orientation at which a counselor is functioning would be reflected by the nature of responses given to the hypothetical ethical dilemmas. Response options for the EJS, reflecting each of the five ethical orientations, are logically-keyed to each alternative of the twenty-five-item scale.

A scoring key is provided with this manual. (See Appendix A.) It should be remembered that the scale essentially measures qualitative differences in ethical orientation with an underlying continuity of ethical reasoning, and therefore, is best conceptualized as descriptive form of measurement.

The scale should be scored in the following manner. The frequency or percentage with which responses are given at each stage of ethical orientation (punishment, institutional, societal, individual, and principle) can be tabulated as an index of counselor orientation at the various levels. Examining the distribution or profile of responses of an individual can provide evidence of the predominant ethical posture of a counselor and the relative levels of functioning. Appendix B provides an example of the scoring format. It should be assumed that most individuals do not solely function at any given level, and those levels are a reflection of many other related variables. Examining the distribution of responses can give an indication of the general level of functioning, that is, the individual's predominant mode of ethical judgment, his or her level of ethical orientation. Thus, for each respondent, a five-point profile or frequency distribution can be obtained with *modal* frequency indicative of the predominant ethical orientation.

Where a more quantitative index is required (e. g. research purposes), the percentage of Stage V responses may be calculated as a useful variable to indicate proportion of higher level ethical reasoning.

Reliability and Validity

Reliability and validity data for the Ethical Judgment Scale are based upon the initial fifteen-item EJS which has been revised to its present twenty-five-item format. It is the authors' belief that the revisions have substantially improved the initial psychometric properties of EJS. Because the revision of the scale was developed parallel to the original scale, the reliability and validity indicated in this section may be considered to be *conservative* estimates of the scale's psychometric properties.

Table 1 presents the means and standard deviations of counselor responses to the five stages of the EJS for various counselor subpopulations.

As can be seen by comparisons of the modal stages, the greater the level of training, the greater the levels of ethical orientations. It should be noted, however, that these data from research conducted on the EJS, should not be taken as normative. Specific norming data have not been undertaken because it has been the authors' intent not to undertake inter-individual comparisons, but rather use the EJS for intra-individual information to aid in self-development of ethical awareness.

Pearson product moment correlation coefficients are among the fifteen items of the EJS presented in Table 2. Generally, the correlations are of a low positive nature with an absence of any significant correlations, suggesting a general consistency across items.

Table 1

Means and Standard Deviations for Counselor Subgoups to the Five Ethical Stages of Ethical Behavior

STAGE	Community College Counselor[a]		Counselor Trainees[b]		Doctoral Students[c]	
	Mean	SD	Mean	SD	Mean	SD
Punishment	1.41	1.73	1.28	1.13	1.10	.93
Institutional	2.99	1.26	1.72	1.48	1.57	1.04
Societal	4.39	1.59	5.02	1.51	3.87	1.43
Individual	3.36	1.26	4.61	1.67	4.68	1.51
Principle	2.86	1.35	2.37	1.92	3.77	1.33

a   n = 174 Vafakas (1972)

b   n = 65 Paradise (1976

c   n = 26

Table 2

Pearson Product Moment Correlation Coefficients for the Ethical Judgment Scale Items[a]

Items	1	2	3	4	5	6	7	8	9	10	11	12	13	14	15
1.	x	.13	.05	.23	.18	.09	.19	.09	.29	.17	.07	.24	.09	.08	.15
2.		x	.14	.01	.08	.18	-.02	.41	.16	.35	.10	-.02	.05	.00	.13
3.			x	.11	.24	.24	.29	.26	.14	.32	.05	.01	.06	.07	.17
4.				x	-.02	.07	-.06	.06	-.09	.24	.00	.08	.18	.04	.03
5.					x	.13	.17	.16	.17	.12	.16	.35	.13	.04	.08
6.						x	.36	.10	.27	.29	.23	.12	.02	.19	.14
7.							x	.26	.16	.32	.33	.18	.12	.23	.14
8.								x	.18	.42	.23	-.04	.02	.12	.09
9.									x	.36	.04	.29	.31	.05	.20
10.										x	.23	.08	.05	.32	.27
11.											x	.16	.12	.14	.24
12.												x	.18	.04	.20
13.													x	.09	.24
14.														x	.17
15.															x

[a]   n = 82 (Paradise, 1976)

In examining the internal consistency of the EJS, Table 3 presents the item-total correlation coefficients for the fifteen items. Coefficient alpha for these data was calculated at .64. Correcting for the length of the revised EJS (Nunnally, 1967), coefficient alpha for the twenty-five-item EJS was determined to be .76. It should be noted that the low correlation items were revised or deleted in the present twenty-five-item EJS.

Table 3

**Item-Total Correlation Coefficients
for Ethical Judgment Scale Items[a]**

EJS Items	Item-Total
1.	.17
2.	.29
3.	.31
4.	.02
5.	.24
6.	.37
7.	.35
8.	.31
9.	.40
10.	.54
11.	.33
12.	.21
13.	.12
14.	.23
15.	.27

[a] n = 82 (Paradise, 1976)

Directly relevant to the validity of the EJS, a correlation matrix of the intercorrelations of the five stages is presented in Table 4. This data was obtained from the same sample as data in Tables 2 and 3 (Paradise, 1976).

Table 4

Intercorrelation Matrix for Ethical Judgments Stages[a]

Ethical Stage	Punishment	Institutional	Societal	Individual	Principle
Punishment	x				
Institutional	.17	x			
Societal	.02	.00	x		
Individual	-.34	-.33	-.40	x	
Principle	-.43	-.51	-.44	-.01	x

[a] n = 82

If the stages of ethical orientation are qualitatively different, as proposed, negative or low positive correlations would be expected. The table confirms this contention. The general tendency for the correlations to diminish as one moves away from the main diagonal, either going down the columns or across the rows should be present. In examining the matrix, there are only two exceptions to the ten relative positions and even these are close to the expected values. The intercorrelations among the stages provide validity for the stage conceptualization of ethical orientation.

Factor analytic data reported by Vafakas (1972) provides additional support for the validity of the stage conceptualization of ethical orientation. A factor analysis on the ethical stage scores for 174 community college counselors using a principle components analyses with varimax rotation yielded the rotated factor matrix presented in Table 5.

Table 5

Varimax Rotated Factor Matrix[a]

| | STAGES | | | |
Stage	Principle	Individual	Institutional	Punishment
Punishment	-0.093	-0.097	-0.097	0.904
Institutional	-0.110	-0.113	0.886	-0.111
Societal	-0.481	-0.414	-0.414	-0.371
Individual	-0.110	0.885	-0.114	-0.111
Principle	0.857	-0.144	-0.143	-0.139

[a] Vafakas (1972)

The data in Table 5 suggest the relative independence of the ethical stages. The factor composition would appear to support the theoretical rationale underlying the instrument. This would indicate support for the construct validity of the EJS: the finding that relatively discrete categories, consistent with the theoretical basis for discriminating various ethical orientations of counselors, would provide support for the general efficacy of the scale.

In the same study, examination of sex differences on ethical orientation yielded no significant relationship between sex of counselor and ethical posture. Additionally, research suggested that the greater the degree of contact with clients, the greater the chance that counselors behaved within an individual or principle orientation; less contact being associated with punishment or institutional orientations. Also, the older the counselor, the more punitive the ethical orientation. Counselors with greater years of counseling experience tended to be more punitive in their orientation than their less experienced colleagues.

Additional research by Paradise (1976), investigating the stage conceptualization of the EJS, demonstrated that the second most frequent ethical stage for an individual is adjacent to the modal or most frequently selected ethical stage at a probability for greater than chance expectation (p < .001). This is important to the construct validity of the EJS for if the stage model is to be valid, it would be expected that an individual's responses would generally center around the dominant orientation and not be randomly distributed across the five ethical orientations.

Paradise (1976) also found a significant relationship between locus of control (Rotter, 1966) and ethical orientation, as predicted: the more internally-oriented, the lower the ethical orientation. Since the higher levels of ethical orientation suggest an underlying rationale of judgment based upon internal principles rather than adherence to externally-determined rules and expectations, it would be expected that greater levels of ethical reasoning would be related to higher levels of internally-perceived control.

Uses for the Ethical Judgment Scale

The EJS was designed primarily as a research tool to examine the ethical orientation of counselors. It is the only instrument, to date, that attempts to examine the ethical posture of counselors and other helping professionals by use of a theoretically-based model of ethical development.

Many areas of research on the ethical behavior of counselors still require investigation. Little research has been undertaken in this important area. Many significant research questions exist. For a discussion of research in the area of ethical behavior see Paradise (1978). It is hoped that ethical orientation as conceptualized by the EJS will aid in the inquiry of the ethical behavior of counselors.

Of perhaps greater importance, the EJS has been used in the ethical training of counselors with encouraging success. Using the scale in small group discussions can enhance the ethical awareness of participants. The hypothetical ethical dilemmas can encourage exploration of the ethical decision-making process and provide insight and understanding of the rationale and reasoning that underlie one's actions in helping situations. The authors have used the scale in workshop activities to encourage discussion and exploration much the same way as Kohlberg (1975) advocates moral education training. To support this use, Paradise (1976) found that using ethical dilemmas as training exercises in small group discussions produced significant increases in the ethical orientation of graduate counseling students when compared to appropriate control groups.

Also, the EJS has been shown to be a useful stimulus for discussion with counseling students as part of regular coursework for techniques and practicum courses in counselor training programs.

Generating additional questions related to the rationale for selected responses as well as using the vignettes as possible role play situations will encourage the depth of exploration and insight needed for ethical development. With slight modification and a little creativity, the EJS can be a beneficial adjunct to counselor training and self-development efforts.

BIBLIOGRAPHY

Dewey, J. What psychology can do for the teacher. In R. Archambault (Ed.), *John Dewey on education: Selected writings*. New York: Random House, 1964.

Kohlberg, L. The development of children's orientations towards a moral order: Sequence in the development of human thought. *Vita Humana*, 1963, *6*, 11-33.

Kohlberg, L. The cognitive developmental approach to education. *Phi Delta Kappan*, 1975, *56*(10), 670-677.

Nunnally, J. *Psychometric theory*. New York: McGraw-Hill, 1967.

Paradise, L. V. Toward a theory on the ethical behavior of counselors. Unpublished doctoral dissertation. University of Virginia, 1976.

Paradise, L. V. What price ethics. New research directions in counselor ethical behavior. *Counseling and Values*, 1978, *23*(1), 2-9.

Piaget, J. *The moral judgment of the child*. New York: Free Press, 1965.

Rotter, J. B. Generalized expectancies for internal versus external control of reinforcement. *Psychological Monographs*, 1966, *80*, No. 1 (Whole No. 609).

Vafakas, K. M. An investigation of some ethical behaviors of community college counselors. Unpublished doctoral dissertation, Wayne State University, 1972.

Vafakas, K. M. Ethical behaviors of community college counselors. *Journal of College Student Personnel*, 1974, *15*(2), 101-104.

Van Hoose, W. H. Some ethical dilemmas of helping professionals. Wayne State University, 1971. (Mimeographed)

Van Hoose, W. H. & Paradise, L.V. Systematic training for the ethical development of counselors. Paper presented to the annual convention of the American Personnel and Guidance Association, Dallas, March 1977.

APPENDIX A

SCORING KEY TO ETHICAL INCIDENTS

STAGES

Incident Number	Punishment	Institutional	Societal	Individual	Principle
1.	A	B	E	C	D
2.	B	A	D	E	C
3.	E	C	A	D	B
4.	B	C	D	A	E
5.	B	A	C	D	E
6.	B	A	D	D	C
7.	E	A	B	E	C
8.	D	C	B	C	A
9.	B	E	A	C	D
10.	D	A	B	D	E
11.	A	B	C	D	E
12.	B	C	A	D	E
13.	D	C	E	A	B
14.	A	C	B	D	E
15.	A	B	D	E	C
16.	A	B	D	C	E
17.	C	C	E	D	A
18.	B	C	E	D	A
19.	A	C	D	E	B
20.	A	B	D	C	E
21.	B	E	D	C	A
22.	D	E	A	C	B
23.	B	A	E	C	D
24.	C	B	E	D	A
25.	A	E	B	C	D

APPENDIX B

Profile Sheet
for Distribution of Counselor's Level
of Orientation for EJS[a]

Percentage of responses
for each category

	Punishment	Institutional	Societal	Individual	Principle
100			25		
80			20		
60			15		
40			10		
20			5		

[a] Modal response is dominant ethical orientation stage.

THE ETHICAL JUDGMENT SCALE

by

William H. Van Hoose, Ph.D.
University of Virginia

and

Louis V. Paradise, Ph.D.
Catholic University of America

INSTRUCTIONS

On the following pages you will find hypothetical incidents involving various helping professionals and the people with whom they work. Each incident is followed by several possible courses of action. Select a response; circle the choice which most closely describes the action you would take in the situation. For certain items, no answer may seem appropriate; in that event please attempt to select the response which is most acceptable to you. There are no *right* or *wrong* answers. Be sure to select only *one* answer.

After you have made a choice, describe the reason for your action, i. e., indicate why you feel the alternative selected is the most appropriate. You may also wish to suggest another course of action or to modify the course of action which you have selected.

Incident One: THE PRISON ESCAPEE

You are a counselor in a community mental health center. A young man who had received short-term counseling from you two years ago, enters your office and explains that he is an escapee from the state prison where he is serving a ten-year term for child molestation. He has been on the run for several months. He appears tired, anxious and scared. He states that he is undecided about his next move: He does not know whether he should leave the country or give himself up.

Counselor Action:

A. Tell him you do not work with criminals and report him immediately to proper authorities.

B. Help him to understand the seriousness of his crimes and counsel him to surrender immediately.

C. Explain that you cannot make his decisions but that you will try to help find possible solutions.

D. Here is a person in trouble — give him help without regard for his behavior or for later consequences.

E. Tell him you will work with him but that he should turn himself in and avoid further trouble.

Why did you select this response? ....

....

....

....

Can you suggest another course of action? If so, please state it, and your reasons. ....

....

....

....

....

Incident Two: SEXUAL SEDUCTION

You are a counselor in private practice. A twenty-eight year old client comes to you complaining that she stopped seeing her previous counselor because he attempted to seduce her. She is afraid to make this known to anyone because her husband is a jealous person and she fears that no one would believe her because of her promiscuous behavior during her adolescent years.

Counselor Action:

A.   Ask the client to give you the counselor's name so that you can report him to the local ethics committee.

B.   Discuss the issue with the client to determine if she contributed, in part, to the actions of the counselor.

C.   Honor the client's wishes about not reporting the counselor's behavior, but discuss the situation in terms of her present motivation and goals for counseling.

D.   Suggest to her that she has grounds for a lawsuit and that her actions may prevent others from being victimized by this counselor.

E.   Discuss the issue with the client in terms of how the incident has affected the client's present emotional state.

Why did you choose this response? ....

....

....

....

....

Can you suggest another course of action? If so, please state it, and give your reasons. ....

....

....

....

....

....

Incident Three: CHILD ABUSE

During a conference with a student's mother, you, as a school counselor, observe that the mother is distraught and anxious. She seems unable to talk about her son, who is the subject of the conference, and begins to express her own feelings and fears. She is pregnant for the fifth time and does not desire to have the child. She states that her frustrations have been "taken out on" her son and that she has physically abused him. She is seeking ways to terminate the pregnancy. Her husband has not been informed of the pregnancy and she is reluctant to tell him.

Counselor Action:

A. Counsel the mother to inform her husband of her condition and give her the names of agencies that can help her.

B. Suggest to her that the termination of the pregnancy may be the best alternative and it is her, and only her decision to make.

C. Explain to the parent that you would like to help but school counselors do not get involved in *family* or medical problems.

D. Help her to consider the seriousness of child abuse.

E. Inform the child abuse authorities that you suspect possible child abuse.

Why did you select this response? ....

....

....

....

Can you suggest another course of action? If so, please state it, and your reasons. ....

....

....

....

....

Incident Four: THE DOUBLE BIND

You are a teacher at a community college. One of your students comes to see you complaining that the department chairman has casually suggested an affair in return for assisting him with his course. The student fears that the professor, who is tenured and your superior, will give her a bad grade if she does not consent.

Counselor Action:

A. Ask the student how she would like you to help and explore possible consequences of these actions.

B. Advise the student to drop the course with the professor, and thus, avoid any embarrassing situations.

C. Suggest that this is a personal problem that should be resolved with the individual since no official rules of the school have been violated.

D. Find out the name of the professor and report it to your supervisor to prevent any further difficulties.

E. Help her resolve the problem without regard for the consequences from your supervisor.

Why did you select this response? ....

....

....

....

Can you suggest another course of action? If so, please state it, and your reasons. ....

....

....

....

....

....

Incident Five: ETHICS AND DRUG ABUSE

A client you have been working with for a period of time explains that he has been taking drugs and really thinks "it is great." He confidentially tells you that the drugs have made him more imaginative and alert. They have increased his thinking but he fears the medical consequences after reading about the dangers of drugs in the newspapers.

Counselor Action:

A.   Immediately direct the young man to a drug center where he can learn to eliminate the habit.

B.   Report his drug activities to the proper authorities.

C.   Reinforce his concern over the danger of taking drugs and encourage him to terminate the practice immediately. Give him additional literature to strengthen his decision.

D.   Help him understand the meaning of his dependency on drugs.

E.   Tell him that some drugs may not really be harmful and suggest that he has a right to "do his own thing."

Why did you select this response? ....

....

....

....

Can you suggest another course of action? If so, please state it, and your reasons. ....

....

....

....

....

....

Incident Six: IS THIS PLAGIARISM?

You are a professor of counseling and you discover that one of your colleagues has taken credit for a report that was written by a student. The student is not aware of the professor's behavior. This is the second occurrence of this type of behavior by this colleague.

Counselor Action:

A.   Forget the incident since it is a matter for the student and faculty member to resolve.

B.   Anonymously report the faculty member to the faculty ethics committee.

C.   Confront the professor with your knowledge of the incident and discuss the possible consequences of the situation with him.

D.   Talk to the chairman of your department about the situation without mentioning the names of the individuals involved.

E.   Discuss the situation with the student involved and assist him in deciding how he would like to handle it.

Why did you select this response? ....

....

....

....

....

Can you suggest another course of action? If so, please state it, and your reasons. ....

....

....

....

....

....

Incident Seven: THE SUICIDE ISSUE

During the course of a session with a counselor, a client admits that he is planning to commit suicide. He is completely disorganized, his school work is failing, he has no friends, and he finds no purpose in continuing the struggle for existence.

Counselor Action:

A.   The counselor should contact the Suicide Prevention Center; it can then attempt to adequately deal with his client's disturbances.

B.   The counselor should try to help his client gain more self-confidence by stressing his strong qualities.

C.   Because of the importance of the situation, his parents or nearest relatives should be contacted immediately.

D.   So that he can learn to interact with young people and share some common interests, the counselor should direct his client to various youth organizations.

E.   The counselor should tell the young man that it is wrong to take any life even one's own. Because the client feels so strongly he should also tell him to seek help from a psychiatrist.

Why did you select this response? ....

....

....

....

....

Can you suggest another course of action? If so, please state it, and your reasons. ....

....

....

....

....

Incident Eight: THE COUNSELOR AND CONFIDENTIALITY

The parents of a seventeen year old girl are planning to sue a counselor for withholding information concerning their daughter's pregnancy and abortion which resulted in severe mental anguish and illness for the daughter.

Counselor Action:

A.   The counselor should stand on the position of client-counselor confidentiality without regard for personal consequences.

B.   The counselor should seek legal advise from colleagues and his professional association, since the counselor may have been partially responsible for the girl's action.

C.   The counselor should convince the parents that the action taken was in good faith.

D.   The counselor can apologize to the parents saying that he did not know what action the girl would take.

E.   The counselor can claim he cannot discuss the situation with the parents without the daughter's permission.

Why did you choose this response? ....

....

....

....

....

Can you suggest another course of action? If so, please state it, and your reasons. ....

....

....

....

....

....

Incident Nine: RIGHTS OF PRIVACY

You are a school counselor. A frightened young lady enters your office and tearfully confesses that she has been promiscuous. She is pregnant and does not know who the father is because she has had numerous affairs. She is without funds and is ashamed to tell her parents about her condition.

Counselor Action:

A. Suggest that you arrange a conference with the parents before any decisions are made.

B. Suggest that legal action could be taken against the various boys who may be responsible for her condition so that the "father" could be made to assume the financial responsibilities.

C. Since time is important, help her to decide if she wishes to go through with the pregnancy or not.

D. Help her to see that she has a right to make any decision she wishes.

E. Inform the young lady that the function of a counselor is not to give medical advice.

Why did you select this response? ....

....

....

....

....

Can you suggest another course of action? If so, please state it, and your reasons. ....

....

....

....

....

Incident Ten: MINORS, MORALS, AND PARENTS

A young man seeks your advice as a counselor in the area of birth control. He is fifteen years of age and is actively engaging in sexual relations. He is tired of his parents meddling into his affairs. He states that his parents are very conservative regarding sexual matters and he is seeking specific information from you.

Counselor Action:

A.   Suggest that premarital sexual relations are wrong and that they can lead to more severe problems like venereal disease, pregnancy, abortion, etc.

B.   Tell the young man that you cannot handle medical problems and that he should seek the advice of a physician.

C.   Help him to understand the meaning and impact of his behavior.

D.   Inform his parents of his promiscuous behavior.

E.   Give him the names of referral agencies that will provide him with appropriate birth control information.

Why did you select this response? ....

....

....

....

....

Can you suggest another course of action? If so, please state it, and your reasons. ....

....

....

....

....

Incident Eleven: BEYOND THE COUCH

One of your clients, who also happens to be a counselor, confesses to you that he has had numerous sexual affairs with his clients. He is feeling guilty about these actions because he fears that someone will find out and he may lose his credentials for private practice.

Counselor Action:

A. Report him to the state credentialing committee.

B. Inform him that you cannot continue seeing him unless he stops this behavior immediately.

C. Discuss with him the potential damage to the clients as a result of his actions.

D. Help him to understand the consequences, both legal and ethical, of his actions.

E. Help him in any way possible to terminate this behavior while warning him that this type of unethical behavior may require you to undertake action to remedy the situation.

Why did you select this response? ....

....

....

....

....

....

Can you suggest another course of action? If so, please state it, and your reasons. ....

....

....

....

....

Incident Twelve: MORALITY AND THEFT

You are a school counselor. In the course of a session, a client admits to stealing a valuable coat from a local store. The manager of the store is a personal friend of yours. The young man admits he took the coat "in a moment of weakness" and wants to rectify the situation.

Counselor Action:

A.　Tell the client to give the coat to you and you will return the coat to the store without revealing his identity.

B.　Have him tell his parents what he has done; then turn him over to the proper authorities so that he will pay his debt to society.

C.　Have the manager of the store come into your office and confront the boy. If the boy is truly sorry for the deed, persuade the manager to give the boy another chance.

D.　The stolen coat is not the real problem and therefore counseling should focus upon why the boy stole the coat.

E.　Tell the boy that the stolen coat is a matter of his own conscience and that you will assist him in any way possible.

Why did you select this response? ....

....

....

....

....

Can you suggest another course of action? If so, please state it, and your reasons. ....

....

....

....

....

Incident Thirteen: HONESTY IN COUNSELING

A college student has taken a personality test given by his counselor and the results indicate a severely distrubed individual. The client wants to know the results of the test.

Counselor Action:

A. Upon questioning the counselor, the student will be told the results were "about normal." The counselor fears that the test results might aggravate the student's emotional condition and increase the disturbance.

B. The true results should be made known to the client because he asked for the testing and has a legitimate right to find out the correct results.

C. The counselor should tell the client not to worry about it and that he cannot give out the results because it is against policy.

D. The student's parents should be notified immediately and proper psychiatric attention should be made available.

E. The client should be directed to a psychiatric facility or agency, for further testing because he might prove dangerous to himself or other students.

Why did you select this response? ....

....

....

....

....

Can you suggest another course of action? If so, please state it, and your reasons. ....

....

....

....

....

Incident Fourteen: SEXUAL ABUSE

During a discussion with a fourteen year old client, you, as a counselor, suspect that she has been sexually abused by friends of her stepfather. However, the client speaks very favorably of her stepfather's friends.

Counselor Action:

A.   Warn the client of the seriousness of this situation and inform the appropriate social agency.

B.   Discuss the situation with the client to determine if anything illegal has occurred.

C.   Inform the client of a counselor's responsibility to report cases of child abuse before she continues to talk about the situation.

D.   Discuss the situation with the client. If the suspicions are correct, discuss possible solutions with the client.

E.   Discuss the situation with the client, helping her to resolve the situation in the manner she wishes.

Why did you select this response? ....

....

....

....

....

Can you suggest another course of action? If so, please state it, and your reasons. ....

....

....

....

....

Incident Fifteen: **THE ABORTION DILEMMA**

You are a college counselor. A young girl, who has just entered her freshman year at the college, seeks your advice. She has been dating a young man for several years and much to her distress, finds herself pregnant. The young man, who is a student, wants to marry her and wants her to have the child. She is undecided about marrying at this time because she is intent on finishing her education and also she does not want the responsibility of a baby.

Counselor Action:

A. Help the girl to consider marrying the young man and having the child. Discuss possible opportunities for continuing her education after the birth of the baby.

B. Tell her that her parents may have to be informed because she is a minor.

C. Since she is opposed to having the child, help her to seek avenues of terminating the pregnancy.

D. Discuss the possible problems resulting from abortion. Direct her to the proper authorities so that she can have the child and then give the infant up for adoption.

E. Arrange a conference with her and the prospective father to discuss possible alternatives and their consequences.

Why did you select this response? ....

....

....

....

Can you suggest another course of action? If so, please state it, and your reasons. ....

....

....

....

....

Incident Sixteen: THE HOMOSEXUAL

A male teenage client come to you, his counselor, in a panic because he has had homosexual encounters with other men. He fears that he will be found out and suspects he has contracted venereal disease because of his casual contacts.

Counselor Action:

A. Help the client to understand his behavior and its possible consequences for his emotional state.

B. Put him in touch with a physician who will handle the case confidentially.

C. Turn him over to the disease control authorities so that his contacts can be traced.

D. Counsel him that his behavior is wrong and sooner or later he will be discovered.

E. Tell him that he has a medical problem that must be resolved before a counselor can work with him.

Why did you select this response? ....

....

....

....

....

....

Can you suggest another course of action? If so, please state it, and your reasons. ....

....

....

....

....

Incident Seventeen: THE "PUSHER"

The counselor is having an interview with a female student concerning the use of drugs. She finally tells the counselor that she knows who is distributing the drugs on the school grounds. She is in love with the boy and will not testify against him because of her affection for him and also because she too is "hooked" on drugs and will have a difficult time obtaining them without her boyfriend's help.

Counselor Action:

A.   Because of the severity of the problem, the authorities should be notified immediately.

B.   The counselor should recommend that the girl turn the boy over to the authorities and point out that help will be given to the girl to get off drugs.

C.   The counselor should not report her but instead should provide counseling to help her understand how her drug problem and boyfriend are affecting her life.

D.   Because of school and legal policies parents of the girl should be notified and the identity of the pusher (must be) revealed before she is allowed to return to school.

E.   The counselor should keep the whole situation quiet and let the drug problem be handled by authorities through different means, because the unfavorable publicity would be embarrassing to the school.

Why did you choose this response? ....

....

....

....

Can you suggest another course of action? If so, please state it, and your reasons. ....

....

....

....

Incident Eighteen: RIGHTS, INTERESTS, AND DUTIES

You are a college counselor. The parents of a former client are requesting information about their son who has left college in his second year and has not informed them of his whereabouts. The parents would like to know the nature of their son's visits in an effort to help locate him.

Counselor Action:

A. Inform the parents that you do not know where the son is now and that you cannot discuss the case unless you have the permission of the son.

B. Since the son has caused considerable anguish for his parents by not following your suggestion to discuss his plans with them, inform the parents of their son's friends who might know his whereabouts.

C. Inform the parents that the nature of the counseling is confidential but you can put them in touch with the dean's office which may be able to help them locate their son.

D. Help the parents to understand the nature of confidentiality and that it was their son's wish to leave without informing them.

E. Inform the parents that their son is of legal age to come and go as he pleases, but that if they are concerned for his safety, they should contact the local police department.

Why did you choose this response? ····························· ·········· ·····························

·········· ··

·········· ··

·········· ··

Can you suggest another course of action? If so, please state it, and your reasons. ···

·········· ············· ···

·········· ··

·········· ··

Incident Nineteen: THE CHILD PROSTITUTE

As a counselor, one of your clients comes to you and explains that she is a prostitute. She has just turned fourteen years old and does not live with her parents. She would like to stop this life, but is afraid. She does not feel her life is worthwhile, but realizes that prostitution is the only means by which she can make the amount of money she requires.

Counselor Action:

A.   Since the client is under age, arrange a conference with her parents and inform them of her behavior.

B.   Explain that she has a right to live her own life and that you will assist her with conflicts which may develop.

C.   Advise her of the dangers of prostitution and attempt to find out how she got into this trouble.

D.   Help her to understand the full legal and religious consequences of her behavior.

E.   Explain that you can accept her but that society will not condone what she does; therefore, offer to provide whatever services you can.

Why did you choose this response? ....

....

....

....

Can you suggest another course of action? If so, please state it, and your reasons. ....

....

....

....

....

....

Incident Twenty: ETHICS AND LAW

A counselor has been working with a client for some time. The client has committed a crime and the counselor has been summoned to court and advised to bring all of the client's records with him.

Counselor Action:

A.   Since the counselor has received a summons, he should comply with the request of the authorities.

B.   The counselor should turn over only basic information saying that these are the only records he has for the client.

C.   Since the records could be damaging to the client, the counselor should destroy or hide them.

D.   The counselor should appear in court without the records claiming that they are confidential.

E.   The counselor should refuse to appear in court because of the confidentiality of the client-counselor relationship.

Why did you choose this response? ....

....

....

....

....

Can you suggest another course of action? If so, please state it, and your reasons. ....

....

....

....

....

....

....

Incident Twenty-one: THE COUPLE

You are a marriage counselor. In counseling a married couple, you have seen the husband and wife individually for several months. When you see them together, the husband continually confronts his wife's accusations that he has been with other women by charging her with paranoia and insecurity. She complains that his womanizing is the only stumbling block in their relationship. You realize that she is correct in her accusations because her husband has admitted his affairs to you during individual counseling sessions. She seeks your assistance.

Counselor Action:

A.   Disregard your knowledge of this situation because it was told to you in confidence.

B.   Inform the wife and husband that she is correct and unless the extramarital affairs stop, the marriage cannot be saved.

C.   Discuss the wife's feelings and attempt to have the husband understand how she could be reacting in this way.

D.   Inform the couple that for counseling to be successful, both must be honest with each other.

E.   Inform the wife that while she has agreed that what she has said in individual counseling is open for discussion, her husband has not agreed.

Why did you choose this response? ....

....

....

....

Can you suggest another course of action? If so, please state it, and your reasons. ....

....

....

....

....

Incident Twenty-two: THE "BAD TRIP"

You are a counselor. A client walks into your office while having a bad trip on drugs. The mind of your client is operating in a framework he has never experienced before; it appears to be at the brink of rage and terror. A lot of bad trippers are convinced that they have gone crazy forever. What do you do?

Counselor Action:

A. Ask the client if he has a friend he would like to see.

B. Convince him that everything is going to be all right. Try to "talk him down" regardless of how long it may take.

C. Take him out of school and walk him around to be sure no one will call the authorities.

D. Immediately call the security guard to help control him.

E. Call his parents and have them pick him up before he hurts himself or someone else.

Why did you choose this response? ....

....

....

....

....

....

Can you suggest another course of action? If so, please state it, and your reasons. ....

....

....

....

....

Incident Twenty-three: INFORMATION GIVING

As a counselor you are asked to write a job recommendation for a former client. The client has signed a release of information form for the prospective employer. However, the recommendation form contains questions related to the client's intellectual and emotional history which could possibly damage the client's chances of obtaining the job.

Counselor Action:

A.   Refuse to complete the recommendation by disregarding the request.

B.   Complete the recommendation to the best of your knowledge without regard for the possible consequences to the client.

C.   Attempt to contact the client informing him that the recommendation form contains questions that should be considered confidential and that the release of information form should not have been signed.

D.   Accede to the client's wishes without divulging any negative or confidential information which could be damaging to the client.

E.   Since the client has signed a release of information form, the prospective employer has a right to be aware of the client's past intellectual and emotional state.

Why did you choose this response? ....

....

....

....

Can you suggest another course of action? If so, please state it, and your reasons. ....

....

....

....

....

Incident Twenty-four: A RIGHT TO COMMIT SUICIDE

A client states that he is planning suicide. His counselor tries convincing him to tell his parents so that they can protect him while he is in his present state. The client refuses.

Counselor Action:

A. The counselor should disregard the client's wishes and convince him to seek help immediately.

B. The counselor should arrange a conference with the parents of the client to see if they are aware of the situation.

C. Since the client refuses his advice, the counselor feels it necessary to terminate the sessions.

D. The counselor should direct the client to the Suicide Prevention Center so that it can attempt to adequately deal with his problem.

E. Through counseling, the counselor should pursue with the client the reasons for the lack of communication with his parents.

Why did you choose this response? ....

....

....

....

....

Can you suggest another course of action? If so, please state it, and your reasons. ....

....

....

....

....

....

Incident Twenty-five: THE JUVENILE OFFENDER

As a counselor, you are requested by the court to see a young girl in an effort to determine if she should remain in her home or be sent away to a juvenile facility. She has been arrested for recruiting young people to make pornographic materials. She has been previously involved in numerous troubles with the juvenile authorities. Her parents are fine, upstanding citizens of the community and request they be allowed one more chance to help her. The only available juvenile facility does not have a good reputation for rehabilitation.

Counselor Action:

A. Recommend that the girl be sent to the juvenile facility since she had had several previous opportunities to reform.

B. Discuss the seriousness of her offense with her and if she appears uncooperative, recommend that she be placed in the juvenile facility.

C. Help her to see the consequences of her behavior and that her past actions may require severe actions by the authorities.

D. Counsel with her and her parents to determine if there is a possibility that they can help her change her behavior.

E. Weigh the seriousness of the circumstances against her feelings of remorse and make your decision as to what is best for her, her family, and the community.

Why did you select this response? ....

....

....

....

Can you suggest another course of action? If so, please state it, and your reasons. ....

....

....

....

....

SUMMARY OF ANSWERS TO INCIDENT SITUATIONS

(As a summary of your responses, circle the letter following each incident description here and digest your reasons for your choice.)

Incident Number and Title	Circled Action	Reasons
1. The Prison Escapee	A B C D	
2. Sexual Seduction	A B C D	
3. Child Abuse	A B C D	
4. The Double Bind	A B C D	
5. Ethics and Drug Abuse	A B C D	
6. Is This Plagiarism?	A B C D	
7. The Suicide Issue	A B C D	
8. The Counselor and Confidentiality	A B C D	
9. Rights of Privacy	A B C D	
10. Minors, Morals and Parents	A B C D	
11. Beyond the Couch	A B C D	
12. Morality and Thrift	A B C D	

Incident Number and Title	*Circled Action*	*Reasons*
13. Honesty and Counseling	A B C D	
14. Sexual Abuse	A B C D	
15. The Abortion Dilemma	A B C D	
16. The Homosexual	A B C D	
17. The "Pusher"	A B C D	
18. Rights, Interests and Duties	A B C D	
19. The Child Prostitute	A B C D	
20. Ethics and Law	A B C D	
21. The Couple	A B C D	
22. The "Bad Trip"	A B C D	
23. Information Giving	A B C D	
24. A Right to Commit Suicide	A B C D	
25. The Juvenile Offender	A B C D